OUR FAULTS:

CONVERSATIONS ON THE STATE OF AFFAIRS IN MODERN BLACK AMERICA

DR. ANTHONY O. VIEGBESIE, PHD

ISBN: 1456461893
ISBN 13: 9781456461898

Library of Congress Control Number: 2010918776
CreateSpace, North Charleston, SC

What Others Are Saying About "Our Faults"

"OUR FAULTS" is one of the most riveting books that I have read in a long time. One moment I was agreeing with Dr. Viegbesie, the next, I was arguing with him. This book challenges parents, teachers, preachers, students and every Black American; which is exactly what he intended to do. How could this African-born American know more about my people, American-born Africans than a lot, perhaps, most Black Americans? This man had the statistics and the research to say, with certainty, what ails Black America. It was as though he were Akbar, Hacker, Kunjufu, Karenga and many other highly respected authoritarians wrapped into one huge volcano. This book is a must read and discuss!

—**Marilyn Dishman,** Retired Educator, Poet & Community Leader

" '*Our Faults'* is a well- written, provocative treatise on social responsibility that takes a bold step into a conversation that will certainly spark meaningful dialogue on broad areas of African Americans' behavior that contribute to the general impoverishment of the African American people. The author has definitely broken new ground in race relation and accountability that will instigate internal evolution in the African American Community".

"Dr. Anthony Viegbesie has touched upon a subject that fuels the emotions of anyone who is sensitive to the state of Modern black America. In this book, he ventures into many aspects of life in black America – social, political, economic, and cultural – in both a philosophical and practical perspective. *"Our Faults"* is a book that validates James Baldwin's statement that 'Not everything that is faced can be changed, but nothing can be changed until it is faced'"

" *'Our Faults'* awakens the consciousness of humanity in general and the African American Community in particular to some of the deductive reasoning/thought processes that contribute to a people's economic demise. Dr. Viegbesie, in this book, has taken a bold step in asking the reader to take a look at the man in the mirror".

Acknowledgments

Many people contributed to the writing and completion of this book. I would like to thank in particular the curious students in my Black Economic Development classes at the Florida Agricultural and Mechanical University in Tallahassee, Florida and the many other students in my economics and public administration classes at both Florida A&M University and Tallahassee Community College in Tallahassee, Florida for their input. Their class discussions and opinion papers have been instrumental in shaping the direction of this book.

I also would like to thank my many friends whose work on the book was indispensable to its completion.

Finally, I have been fortunate to have my family's support and prayers to have the motivation and determination I needed to write this book.

Dedication

This book is dedicated to my mother, the late Mrs. Lady Ahwinahwi (Nee Uwanjovo), the strongest woman I have ever known to walk the face of this earth. My mother, whose teachings have given me the wisdom and whose prayers and blessings have guided me to the grace of God. She is why I am who and what I have become today.

I truly thank God for sending me to this world and giving me the privilege and honor of being your child. Your prayers continue to manifest themselves in my life. My mother taught me to believe that I am the best thing that God has created and as such should never settle for anything less than the best.

This book is also dedicated to the other two important women in my life, my wife, Diane Viegbesie and daughter, Ediri Viegbesie. These women are the winds beneath my wings. They give me a reason to want to soar to greater heights.

Contents

Introduction

There is a general understanding all over the world that the United States of America has attained the highest stage of economic development to become the richest nation in recorded history. However, there remain sub-communities that are markedly underdeveloped when compared with the rest of the country, and in which the most abject poverty is visible everywhere. One of the sub-communities that has not kept pace with the economic progress of the country as a whole and which, in many important respects, progress has bypassed is the African-American Community. This book is an attempt to address the phenomenon of multi-generational poverty that is common in the African American community.

Recent U.S. Census Bureau data on poverty in America has revealed that a record 43.6 million people now live in poverty and 9.9 million of them are blacks. Data also show that blacks have experienced more than

1 percentage increase in the number of individuals in poverty between 2008 and 2009. Today's data show that about 26 percent of blacks live below the federal poverty line.

The National Urban League's 2010 *The State of Black America* report shows that:

> Unemployment numbers are most troubling. Black unemployment was 14.8 percent in 2009, compared to 12.1 for Hispanics and 8.5 percent for whites. These numbers are significant as the lack of jobs for minorities' means less opportunity for home ownership, less access to healthcare and fewer people engaging in post-secondary education. In many of the categories in the report, blacks either made no progress or lost ground. Whatever small gains made in median household income, since 2005 when the League started conducting these studies, decreased in the 2010 report, falling from 65 percent to 62 percent. Less than half of black and Hispanic families owned homes and both were more than three times as likely as whites to live below the poverty line.

The report also shows a big difference in 2009 real median household income and education level between whites and minorities. Real median income was $34,218 for blacks, $37, 913 for Hispanics and $55,530 for whites. In education, whites over the age of 25 were more than 1½ times as likely as blacks and 2½ times as likely as Hispanics to hold a bachelor's degree. For the first time, *The State of Black America* report, which measures disparities between blacks and whites in areas of economics, education, health, civic engagement and social justice, includes a Hispanic index. While blacks still lag behind, with an overall Equality Index of 75.5 percent, Hispanics are faring better than blacks, with an overall Equality Index of 76.8 percent. By the way, an equality index of less than 100% suggests blacks are doing worse relative to whites, while an index greater than 100% suggests blacks are doing better.

Most recently, the U.S. Census Bureau studies showed that the home ownership rate for blacks dropped from about 50 percent, its peak in 2004 during the boom, to 47 percent in 2006 following the housing market burst. Furthermore, the Center for Responsible Lending data also revealed that the private sector's predatory lenders actually targeted black homeowners by steering them more toward high-cost and high-risk subprime loans than whites with similar credit scores. This meant that black mortgages were less likely to refinance, and were more likely be foreclosed than whites.

Furthermore, a report released by the Pew Research Center on July 26, 2011, states that according to an analysis of new Census data, the wealth gaps between whites and minorities have grown to their widest levels in a quarter-century. The recent recession and uneven recovery have erased decades of minority gains, leaving whites on average with 20 times the net worth of blacks and 18 times that of Hispanics. The report also revealed that the median wealth of white U.S. households in 2009 was $113,149, compared with $6,325 for Hispanics and $5,677 for blacks. Those ratios, roughly 20 to 1 for blacks and 18 to 1 for Hispanics, far exceed the low mark of 7 to 1 for both groups reached in 1995, when the nation's economic expansion lifted many low-income groups to the middle class. And that the white-black wealth gap is also the widest since the census began tracking such data in 1984, when the ratio was roughly 12 to 1.

Rhonda Tsoi-A-Fatt pointed out that:

"The disproportionate percent of African-Americans living in poverty in America is not a new phenomenon. It's been an issue that civil rights advocates and others have long tried to remedy. Living in impoverished communities and families is stressful and costly in the short-term, and produces negative outcomes in the long-term. Poor children and youth are less likely to graduate from high school, more likely to be teen parents, and less likely to be employed as young adults".

She went on to say that:

"What I find most telling, however, is that for black children, being poor in childhood is a significant predictor of poverty in early adulthood. This phenomenon is not the same for white children. A recent Urban Institute study that examined longitudinal data from 1968 to 2005 found that only six percent of white children who were poor at birth were living in poverty as young adults, compared to 41 percent of African Americans".

She recommends that "We need to be more intentional and more vocal about a particular focus on struggling African-Americans and distressed communities of color in America. This is driven, in part, by the fact that black young adults who were born in poverty are less likely to be employed than whites who grew up in the same situation. This is particularly true for males. There is a 62 percentage point difference between rates of consistent employment between white and African American males who grew up in poverty. Additionally, African-American males growing up in impoverished communities are far less likely than their peers to complete high school - oftentimes less than a third get a diploma". (Tsoi-A-Fatt, 2010)

This book is a conversation on the impact of social responsibility on the inner dynamics of an ethnic community in America. Simply stated, the premise of this book is straightforward: a socio-political commentary on the state of black America's actions and beliefs and the lack of communal responsibility and how they contribute to the lack of progress in the black community. It is written to address some of the behaviors of blacks that may be contributing to their own demise.

I don't dare to think that I am knowledgeable enough to propose solutions to the behaviors written about in this book. I believe that there are many other people, in the black community in particular and America in general, who have the wisdom, knowledge, political vastness and religious competence to do just that. The purpose of *Our Faults: Conversations on the State of Affairs in Modern Black America* is to accentuate some of the behaviors or activities of black America that may have contributed and may continue to contribute to the poor socioeconomic conditions that pervade the black communities. The intent of this book is not to provide recommendations for solutions to the identified activities and behaviors per se. Rather, it is this book's intent to point out these behaviors and activities and thus open the door to a dialogue on them.

I am aware of the fact that daring to write on this topic could make me unpopular among some black people and even attract hatred and hostility. Some people in the black community may want to vilify me and call me out of my name. Discussing issues of this nature is considered taboo in the black communities and should be avoided completely. It is human nature to be defensive when we feel that our obvious weaknesses and faults are being revealed to us. It is very important to point out at this juncture that this story of African American self-impoverishment can be equally applied to any other group of impoverished people in any part of the world. It is also important to mention that the observations presented in this book are not, in any way, exclusive to the

African American population; it would be naïve of me to think so.

It is my conviction that since other ethnic groups are busy addressing the issues pertaining to their community development, it is imperative that we also get serious about addressing our own (black American) issues of economic underdevelopment. If we do not address our own problems, who else do we expect to do so for us? I would like to begin by saying that the causes of poverty in the African American community can be argued to be both structural and behavioral. I hope that this book triggers a conversation on these issues, thereby initiating changes that will begin to reduce, if not eliminate, the problem of poverty and hunger in the African American communities.

There are as many opinions as to why African Americans are regarded as an underclass in a nation of plenty as there are people willing to talk about the subject. I am by no means suggesting that all African Americans are poor. After all, *Black Enterprise* magazine revealed that between 1973 and 1994, the current-dollar revenues of the top one hundred African American-owned industrial companies rose from $473 million to $6.7 billion plus $4.9 billion in revenues from auto dealerships. As a matter of fact, African Americans have far outperformed people in any society with a substantial black population.

Andrew Hacker, in his book *Two Nations: Black and White, Separate, Hostile, Unequal*, points out that black Americans are Americans, yet they still subsist as aliens in the only land they know. He further stated that other groups may remain outside the mainstream—some religious sects, for example—but they do so voluntarily. In contrast, blacks have had to endure a segregation that is far from freely chosen. So, America may be seen as two separate nations. Of course, there are places where these races mingle. Yet in most significant respects, the separation is pervasive and penetrating. As a social and human division, it surpasses all others—even gender—in intensity and subordination. America, he said, is inherently a "white" country in structure and in culture. Nevertheless, black Americans create lives of their own. Black American children are almost three times as likely as whites to grow up in poor surroundings. He affirms that after other factors have been accounted for, race still seems to play a role in how people fare economically (Hacker, 2003).

Derrick Bell, in his book, *Faces at the Bottom of the Well: The Permanence of Racism*, states that the racism that made slavery feasible was far from dead in the last decades of twentieth-century America; and the civil rights gains, so hard won, were being steadily eroded. Despite undeniable progress for many, no African American is insulated from incidents of racial discrimination. Our careers, even our lives, are threatened because of our color. Even the most successful of us are haunted by the plight of our less fortunate brethren who struggle for existence in what some social scientists call the "underclass." Burdened with life-long poverty and soul-devastating despair, they live beyond the pale of the American Dream. What we designate as "racial progress" is not a solution to that problem. It is a regeneration of the problem in a particular perverse form. He therefore believes that black people will never gain full equality in the United States. This position conforms to the fundamental ideology that racial preference of white majority will continue to be beyond the reach of the law, even if the procedures of government are formally neutral in racial matters (Bell, 1992).

While facts might be useful in explaining some phenomena, it is important that imagination and intuition come to play in presenting a contentious topic of this magnitude. It is virtually impossible for anyone to come up with a concise explanation for why African-Americans dominate or are disproportionately represented at the bottom socioeconomic class in the United States. I believe that if we, as an ethnic group, begin to address the contributing factors we will begin to see how our actions, our self-image, our world view, and others' perceptions of us are creating our situation then we might begin to do things differently so as to get us out of this bowl of poverty.

Poverty is a very fragile and explosive subject that most people often shy away from for fear of disturbing the status quo. Mahatma Ghandi once said that "Poverty is the worst form of violence." The truth of the matter is that denial prevents people from accepting responsibility for their predicaments or acknowledging that the problems even exist. This book is my attempt to provide a logical explanation for how some black Americans' behaviors contribute to their own economic demise. And I hope that the conversations, as presented, will enable the reader to interact with the book.

Soul searching, rather than playing the blame game, may be inevitable for altering an existing behavior in order to provide the solution to our problems. There has been continuous debate in this country over whether or not the government's actions or inactions should be held accountable for the African American socio-economic predicament. This book and some of the views in it may offend or even vex some readers, especially some in the black communities. Some readers may call for my crucifixion for "selling out." Some may even say, "How dare him?" and "Who does he think he is to think that he is qualified to write on this topic?" Some people may even go as far as accusing me of pandering to or validating the right wing conservative's ideologies. On the other hand, this book may excite and encourage some readers and inspire them to create changes in their lifestyles.

I honestly hope that this book will get the reader thinking about and even starting conversations about those things that we, as blacks, do to contribute to the problem of poverty in our black communities. We seem to subscribe to a culture of accepting poverty as a way of life. Each of the seven chapters in this book will focus on some broad areas of African American behavior that contribute to the general impoverishment of the African American people. I believe that one of the most effective ways African Americans can resolve the issue of poverty in our communities and dig ourselves out of the trenches of the underclass is to speak truth to how some of our own actions have contributed to our own demise. Acknowledging the existence of a problem is the first step toward finding solutions to the problem. I am convinced that becoming aware of how we contribute to our own poverty is enough prescription for changing the economic course of our lives for the better. All I am saying is that we must not forget the enemy within us; the solutions to our problems are sometimes within us. It's time for us to talk about ourselves, as a family—to talk about the things we do to make us suffer in a nation of plenty. Let's talk about those things we do to contribute to our own state of economic poverty.

CHAPTER ONE

Self-Image

"Trust yourself. Create the kind of self that you will be happy to live with all your life. Make the most of yourself by fanning the tiny, inner sparks of possibility into flames of achievement."

—Golda Meir

"Always be a first-rate version of yourself, instead of a second-rate version of somebody else."

—Judy Garland

Our life is like a meal and we are the cook. We are responsible for identifying the dish we plan to prepare, and then determining the correct proportions of the necessary ingredients to make it taste the way we want it to. The ingredients we put into it very much determine how the dish turns out.

Knowing our purpose in life is like identifying the dish we want to prepare. In order to achieve in life, we have to know who we are and identify our goals before coming up with the plans to achieve those goals. Our ability to define our goals depends, to a great extent, on our self-perception. The way we see ourselves determines our level of motivation, confidence, and subsequent success in life. This reminds me of the story of the "pendulum theory" that I was told by my faculty advisor when I was a graduate student at the University of Kentucky. The story was told to me during our meeting to plan my next move upon graduating with a master's degree in agricultural economics.

During this conversation my advisor asked me if I were planning to stay in the United States or return to my country of origin upon graduation. I told him that I was planning on returning to my home country of Nigeria because I was afraid of not being able to attain my fullest potential as a result of my skin color or national origin. It was at this point that he proceeded to tell me about this "pendulum theory." He started by informing me that I was different from black people born in the United States. I must confess that I was confused at first, and then it dawned on me that he might have thought he was actually giving me a complement by telling me of what a different caliber of black I am from those born in the U.S.

When I asked him to explain what he meant by my being different from blacks born in the United States, his response was that mainstream America sees blacks born in Africa as being at an extreme end of a continuum, with white people at the other extreme. He said that those occupying the two extremes are seen as superior groups of people. On one end of the spectrum, he explained, are white people—white in color and white in culture. They know exactly who they are and what they want in life.

On the other end, he continued, are black people born in Africa—black in color and black in culture. They too know exactly who they are and what they want in life. Then, he said, come the blacks born in America; they are black in color and white in culture, confused about exactly who they are, swinging back and forth like a pendulum, and as such do not know who they are or what they really want out of life. He went on to say that African Americans' lack of self-identity explains their lack of focus and purpose in life. Needless to say, I did not find his comments or explanations amusing. However, I took that moment as a learning opportunity.

Arnold M. Ludwige wrote,

"We often speak of one's personal identity as what makes one the person one is. Your identity in this sense consists roughly of what makes you unique as an individual and different from others. Or it is the way you see or define yourself, or the network of values and convictions that structure your life. This individual identity is a property (or set of properties). Presumably it is one you have only contingently—you might have had a different identity from the one you in fact have—and one that you might have for a while and then lose: you could acquire a new individual identity, or perhaps even get by without one". (Ludwige,1997).

Self-image is in large part a social by-product, determined by the attitudes and behavior of others toward the individual. Since many American ethnic groups have been the victims of prejudice, it has been assumed that low self-esteem may result from minority status (Porter and Washington, 1979).

Unfortunately, this belief that Africans born outside the United States are better than Africans born in America is actually shared by a vast majority of African Americans that I have been in contact with. It is common to hear blacks born in America say to blacks born outside United States, "You don't understand that you are different from us. Ya'll are raised in a different culture which is why ya'll are able to do things the way y'all do things." As a matter of fact, some African Americans sometimes become very angry and hostile toward blacks who immigrated to the United States. I have personally and very frequently been referred to as "dawn foreigner" (meaning a transplant from another country) by some of my black American friends, even though they are quite aware that I am now a citizen of the United States. Some blacks have actually accused me and my family of selling their ancestors into slavery and now having come to America to benefit from the hard work of their enslaved ancestors.

It is only when the past and present are fully understood that can we expect to plan effectively for the future. I believe that all of the economic, cultural, political, ideological, and self-identity confusion that exists in black America today are rooted in the philosophical tension between assimilation and isolation that has existed ever since African people were enslaved in America. It is my position that not until the full extent of slavery's damaging impact on the social and economic conditions of Africans born in the United States is completely revealed and understood, African-Americans may never be able to effectively plan for the future.

The dehumanization of people during slavery was a conscious effort to replace the African personality with a slavery mentality—a belief in one's own inferiority and in the superiority of those doing the enslavement. Let us not forget about the racist sentiments that emerged from the institution of slavery, that were embedded in the constitutional documents underlying this country's existence and were quite naturally deeply implanted in the minds of the American people.

Iyanla Vanzant once said that "far too many blacks fail to take the time to ask themselves three very important questions: Who was I? Who am I? Who do I choose to be?" She went on to say that "without so much as a vague answer, a hint about your involuntary responses to these questions, you cannot move beyond the chaos and confusion of daily survival." She wrote that asking *"Who was I?"* gives one a sense of history. Not just one's story—but history of one's skills, talents, and abilities. It is this kind of self-reflection that enables someone to take inventory of his or her life.

She, like me, believes that reflection empowers a person. A close and careful review of "from whence you came" gives you the power to make new choices in life. Asking the question "Who am I?' is taking a look at the blueprint of your life so that you can determine what you must do to accomplish your life's purpose. She further points out that "it takes a great deal of courage to ask yourself, 'Who am I?' and rely on the circumstances and conditions of your life to provide the answers. It is also by asking this question that you can determine whether the life you are living is an accurate testimony of yourself. Your life will tell you the absolute truth about you. The question is, are you willing to hear it?" (Smiley, 2001)

African Americans as a people have, for too long, allowed other people's perceptions of them dictate how they perceive themselves. Living a life without knowing who you are is like starting on a journey without knowing what your destination is. This lack of self-identity is manifested in the way many blacks make their choices in life: the way they choose their friends, the way they decide what is important in life, the way they spend their money and time, et cetera.

Here is a story of a student I had in one of my classes at Florida A&M University who came to me towards the end of the semester because he was failing the course. His concern was that if he did not pass this class he would be suspended on academic grounds since he was already on academic probation. He started by proudly informing me that he is the first in his family to have ever gone to college and flunking out would be a disgrace to him and his family. The problem was that I really did not recognize him as a student in the class because he rarely attended class. When I looked at my class roster I discovered that he had stopped attending class by the end of the first week but came to class only on testing days. When I asked him if he was reading the assigned chapters in the required textbook, since he was not attending class, his response was that he was unable to afford the text book. Let me point out that he was looking good in all of his designer clothes and was holding an iPhone. He also informed me that he was on student financial aid. Furthermore, my class roster showed that the time he stopped attending classes happened to coincide with when students' financial aid checks were disbursed.

Later on during the semester, I came to learn that this same student had been arrested for possession of drugs with the intent to distribute and had just been recently released on bail awaiting trial. Talking with him about life in general revealed how much his focus was more on what kind of clothes he wore and what kind of automobile he drove rather than what he really wanted to make of his life. His appearance, he pointed out, was what determined the level of his success and ultimately how much respect he got in his community. "After all," he said, "when I go back home in my nice truck and looking good, people respect me and they want to be my friends."

Na'im Akbar says it all when he writes that the ultimate effectiveness of any group of people is the degree to which they have an awareness of who they are and respect themselves. Two of the major deficiencies of the African American community are the persistence of a fundamental lack of self-awareness and a debilitating deficit of self-esteem. These characteristics are not new for the African American community, but are deeply rooted in a tradition that was devised to sabotage our collective and personal efficacy and make us into a permanent servant class in America. All of the cultural and institutional devices that are usually employed to ensure that people will develop an effective self-awareness were systematically uprooted and/or prohibited in the African American community during and after slavery. The consequence, he points out, is that African Americans are badly handicapped in competition with other groups of people who are equipped with these fundamental qualities of self-awareness and self-respect (Smiley, 2001). The absence of self-knowledge can lead to people being trapped in a self-defeating pattern of behavior that creates a tangle of social pathologies associated with the underclass.

Too many African Americans are still ashamed to acknowledge the fact that slavery is an integral part of their people's and their country's history. This denial will continue to interfere with our ability to fully come to terms with who we are as a people. As a matter of fact, many African American parents typically do not want to discuss the past at home with their children.

There are African Americans who still believe that black people had little history besides the subjugation and bondage of slavery and therefore are ashamed to talk about slavery at the family dinner table. I wonder how many Africans born in America really know that the first Africans to settle in the United States arrived in South Carolina in 1526, ninety-three years before the Mayflower docked. As a matter of fact, Africans traveled to North America to trade long before the Middle Passage to slavery started.

Now, let's talk a little history of slavery. In the early 1600s, England was eager to gain a colonial foothold on the North American continent. In June of 1606, King James I granted a charter to a group of London entrepreneurs, the Virginia Company. On May 14, 1607, the Virginia Company explorers landed on Jamestown Island to establish the Virginia English colony on the banks of the James River, sixty miles from the mouth of the Chesapeake Bay. It was in 1619, not long after the first settlement, that the need for colonial labor was bolstered by the importation of African captives.

At first, like their poor English counterparts, the Africans were treated as indentured servants, who would be freed of their obligations to their owners after serving for several years. However, over the course of the century, a new race-based slavery system developed, and by the dawn of the new century, the majority of Africans and African Americans had become slaves for life. The popular conception of a race-based slave system did not develop until the 1680s. It was at this time that control over the captive population became a significant issue, and whites' obsessive fear of a slave rebellion began to spread. Many of our ancestors lived without freedom as indentured servants in what historian John Hope Franklin called "the peculiar institution of American slavery". (Franklin, 1947).

Social science literature of the 1920s–1940s, which investigated the effects of marginal status on feelings of personal insecurity (Stonequist, 1937; Lewis, 1948), established a relationship between minority status and low self-esteem. Furthermore, discussions about European immigrant populations touched on the notion of personal disorganization and in-group rejection. This notion has also been applied to the analysis of personality patterns of blacks (Dollard 1937, Johnson 1967).

Many African Americans are not aware that blacks have significantly impacted the development of the social, economic, and political structures of the United States and the world. Too many African Americans now suffer from a particular strand of AIDS (Acquired Inferiority Deficiency Syndrome). It is important for African Americans to know that understanding the history of slavery is central to understanding the history of black people and of the United States.

What amazes me most is how commonplace it is to hear African Americans quickly dismiss any conversation that has to do with slavery. As a matter of fact, there are some black Americans who don't believe that slavery ever existed; they think it is a myth.

Some African Americans are quick to say, "I was not a slave and none of my parents were slaves. Slavery happened so long ago, why must we continue to dwell on the past? Let's get over the past and move forward." For example, Dr. William Cosby once said that "We are not Africans. Those people are not Africans; they don't know a thing about Africa. I say this all of the time—it would be like white people saying they are European-American—that is totally stupid. I was born here, and so were my parents and grandparents and, very likely my great grandparents. I don't have any connection to Africa, no more than white Americans have to Germany, Scotland, England, Ireland, or the Netherlands. The same applies to 99 percent of all the black Americans as regards to Africa—so stop, already!" (Cosby, 2004). I am quite sure that Dr. Cosby had heard white Americans refer to themselves as Irish-American, German-American or Scottish-American, Italian-American, ec cetera. I believe that Africans born in America have the rights to claim the entire continent of Africa because slavery deprived them the knowledge of exactly which African country their ancestors were stolen from.

African Americans' reluctance to accept their history and become comfortable with talking about it reminds me of a story I once heard Rev. Al Sharpton tell about a singer called Clara Ward and her daughter Laura. In this story, Clara had worked very hard, all her life, to send her daughter to college. Her only dream was to give this daughter of hers the education that she never had herself.

Before Laura graduated from high school, Clara was able to save enough money to send her daughter to one of the finest colleges but did not have enough money to enable her daughter to come home on breaks and holidays. So the daughter had to stay at school even during the summer months. And for four whole years Clara never saw her daughter. But her daughter would write home every week. So for four long years their communication was through letters.

Now, after four years, Clara finally got a letter from her daughter stating that she had graduated with her B.S. degree in History. Laura informed her mother of the day she would be coming home and the time of the bus arrival. Early in the morning of the day of her daughter's arrival Clara, full of excitement, got up and made it to the bus depot at about 6 a.m. even though the bus wasn't expected to arrive until 10 a.m. Somewhere between 9 a.m. to 9.30 a.m., all of the other parents began to arrive at the bus depot with their friends and family members to see their sons and daughters come home from school.

Finally, after a while Clara looked up and saw the bus coming. Excitement jumped into her bosom and she could hardly contain herself, looking forward to finally seeing her daughter after four long years. Her daughter for whom she had labored; the pride and joy of her life.

When the bus arrived, and the passengers began to get off, the sons and daughters of other families got off and ran to hug and kiss their parents and family members, but Clara's daughter was nowhere. It was when the bus was almost empty that Laura came down the steps and as Clara ran to throw her arms around her daughter, the daughter walked away in a hurry. Clara ran after her daughter for about two blocks before her daughter finally stopped and turned around to embrace the mother.

They went home without saying anything to one another. At home, they sat down to eat what Clara had woken up earlier to prepare. As they sat down to eat together for the first time in four years, the mother asked the daughter to explain her actions down at the bus station when she got down from the bus and ignored her, acting as if she didn't even know who she was and refusing to acknowledge her presence.

Laura, with her head bowed, said, "Mama, I didn't mean to hurt your feelings. I just didn't want the people I went to school with to know that you were my mother. I just haven't been able to get over that ugly scar on your face. I wanted to hug and kiss you in private. Because the scar on your face is so ugly that I did not want the kids to know that a pretty girl like me had a mother with an ugly scar like that."

It was at this juncture that the mother said to the daughter, "Let me tell you a story I have never told you before: the story of how I got this scar."

She told her daughter, "I was out in the backyard one day hanging clothes on the line when I turned around, and noticed that our house was on fire. Some neighbors who came to help put out the fire suggested that I call the fire department, but I screamed at them, saying "my baby is inside the house!" Without hesitating, I grabbed some clothes from the clothesline, covered my face with them, ran through the flames into the house, and headed straight to the crib where you were lying. I snatched you out of the crib and covered you with those clothes that I had covered my face with when I ran in to get you out of the fire.

It was on my way back out, running through the blazing fire, that I got burnt in the face. You see, I got this scar not from free-basing cocaine during an after-hours clubbing event; I got this scar trying to get you out of the blazing fire unscarred." African Americans are, in too many instances, ashamed to acknowledge themselves as belonging to a beautiful race of people. They must not be ashamed of their scars, but learn to turn those scars into stars.

Another example to show how blacks have a problem with accepting who they are and being proud of it was the 1939 *Clark Doll Experiment*. This experiment validates the dislike that blacks have for being blacks in America. In the experiment, Dr. Kenneth Clark and his wife Mamie showed black children between the ages of six and nine two dolls, one white and one black; the dolls were similar except for their skin color. Then they asked the children these questions in this order (note: "Negro" and "colored" were both common words for blacks before the 1960s):

- "Show me the doll that you like best or that you'd like to play with."
- "Show me the doll that is the 'nice' doll."
- "Show me the doll that looks 'bad.'"
- "Give me the doll that looks like a white child."
- "Give me the doll that looks like a colored child."

- "Give me the doll that looks like a Negro child."
- "Give me the doll that looks like you."

By the last question, most black children had already picked the black doll as the bad one. Their 1950 study revealed that 44% of these black children said the white doll looked like them! In some earlier tests, they noted that many children would refuse to pick either doll or just start crying and run away.

In one study, the Clarks gave the test to 300 children in different parts of the country. They found that black children who went to segregated schools (those separated by race) were more likely to pick the white doll as the nice one than black children in unsegregated schools. In the test that they did that became part of *Brown v Board of Education,* they gave the test to sixteen black children in 1950 in Clarendon County, South Carolina. Of these, 63% said the white doll was the nice one, the one they wanted to play with. Clark also asked the children to color a picture of themselves. Most of the children chose a shade of brown markedly lighter than themselves. In 1954, in *Brown v Board of Education,* this experiment helped to persuade the American Supreme Court that "separate but equal" schools for blacks and whites were anything but equal in practice and therefore against the law. It was the beginning of the end of Jim Crow law of school segregation.

In 2005, Kiri Davis repeated the Clarks' experiment in Harlem as part of her short but excellent film, *A Girl Like Me.* She asked twenty-one children, and 71% of the children told her that the white dolls were the nice one. Not a huge sample size, true, but it was still shocking to see how easily many chose the white doll.

Dombeck and Wells-Moran pointed out that "people's identity is rooted in their identifications; in what they associated themselves with. What a person associates him or herself with is ultimately who that person is, for all identity is ultimately in relationship to something else. An American person identifies himself or herself as 'American,' for example, and that becomes part of that American person's identity. The same person might identify themselves as male (or female), a member of a particular religious group, a brother or sister, a child, an employee, etc." They went on to state that:

> [E]ven more personally, people may identify themselves as a loser, as someone who is helpless to influence the course of their lives, or as someone who needs to hate a particular religious group simply because that is what members of their own religious group are "supposed" to do. Though such personal beliefs may have no basis in reality, they often are taken at face value by the people who hold them. Such people act on their mistaken or irrational beliefs and end up creating problems for themselves. Identity is not just what you know; it is also how you know what you know. People are not born with an identity. Rather,

identity is something that evolves over time. Young children have simple identities and see things in an overly simple, generally self-serving manner. As people grow older and supposedly wiser, they identify themselves with other people, places, and things in increasingly sophisticated ways and start to grow out of this initial selfishness. A young child may see her mother as a creature that exists solely to take care of her, but an older child will often start to appreciate that her mother has needs of her own, and start acting less selfishly towards her mother so as to take that knowledge into account. Sometimes life events interrupt this natural progression from selfishness to thoughtfulness and people's identities stop growing. Such people may be chronologically adults, but relate to others in the selfish manner characteristic of a younger child, creating problems for themselves and the people around them when their selfish expectations clash with those held by people around them, who expect a more adult, more "responsive" and "responsible" identity to be present. Whether due to mistaken beliefs or developmental delays, identity problems can cause people to have

difficulty taking an appropriate perspective towards other important life tasks,
creating a wide range of life problems.
(Dombeck and Wells-Moran, 2006).

I am reminded of a poem written by an unknown artist entitled *LORD, WHY DID YOU MAKE ME BLACK?*
The artist writes:

"Lord, Lord, Why did You make me
Black? Why did You make me someone
the world wants to hold back?

Black is the color of dirty clothes; the
color of grimy hands and feet.
Black is the color of darkness; the color of
tire-beaten streets.

Why did you give me thick lips, a broad
nose and kinky hair?
Why did You make me someone who
receives the hatred stare?

Black is the color of a bruised eye when
somebody gets hurt.
Black is the color of darkness. Black is
the color of dirt.
How come my bone structure's so thick;
my hips and cheeks are high?
How come my eyes are brown and not the
color of the daylight sky?

Why do people think I'm useless? How come I feel so used?
Why do some people see my skin and think I should be abused?

Lord, I just don't understand; What is it about my skin?
Why do some people want to hate me and not know the person within?

Black is what people are "listed", when others want to keep them away.
Black is the color of shadows cast. Black is the end of the day.

Lord, You know, my own people mistreat me;
and I know this just isn't right. They don't like my hair or the way I look.
They say I'm too dark or too light.

Lord, Don't You think it's time for You to make a change?
Why don't You re-do creation and make everyone the same?

(God answered :)

Why did I make you black? Why did I make you black?

Get off your knees and look around. Tell
Me, what do you see?
I didn't make you in the image of dark-
ness. I made you in the Likeness of ME!

I made you the color of coal from which
beautiful diamonds are formed.
I made you the color of oil, the black-gold
that keeps people warm.

I made you from the rich, dark earth that
can grow the food you need.
Your color's the same as the panther's,
known for beauty and speed.

Your color's the same as the Black stal-
lion, a majestic animal is he.
I didn't make you in the Image of darkness, I made you in the Likeness of ME!

All the colors of a Heavenly Rainbow can
be found throughout every nation; And
when all those colors were blended well,
YOU   BECAME   MY   GREATEST
CREATION.

Your hair is the texture of lamb's wool,
such a humble, little creature is he.
I am the Shepherd who watches them. I
am the One who will watch over thee.

You are the color of midnight-sky, I put
the stars' glitter in your eyes.
There's a smile hidden behind your pain
that's the reason your cheeks are high.

You are the color of dark clouds formed
when I send My strongest weather.
I made your lips full so when you kiss the
one you love they will remember.

Your stature is strong; your bone structure,
thick to withstand the burdens of time.
The reflection you see in the mirror...
The Image looking back at you is MINE!"

A poor sense of self-worth (also known as poor
self-esteem) occurs when one comes to believe that
one has little value or worth. This often occurs when
key people in a person's life are critical towards them,
or when a person is a perfectionist and self-critical.
In either case, the tendency is to harshly judge, and
ignore or downplay the importance of real accomplishments, even when it makes no sense to act this
way. There may also be a belief present to the effect
that self-worth can only be based on the acclaim of
other "popular," high status people, even though this is
not the case (Dombeck and Wells-Moran, 2006). This
search for self-worth probably explains why many
African American youths are easily attracted to gang
membership.

"Today's gang membership gives African American youth, who have low self-esteem, a sense of love and respect from gang members. Youth whose self-esteem has been damaged by parents, peer rejection, and school failures may find new identity and self-worth through being in the gang. Joining a gang is also a way for youth to achieve status, as well as self-importance" (Yablonsky, 1962).

This reminds me of a conversation I had with a young man when I visited one of the local high schools in the Tallahassee, Florida area. I was at this school to talk with a group of young people about the negative impacts of gang membership. After I had spilled my guts about all of what I think is bad about gang membership, I asked them to tell me what they thought of our talk. This was when a young man raised his hand, and after I acknowledged him he said, "When I see people walking around wearing their gang colors. I think they're cool. I mean, nobody would even think of messing with them. When I walk in the room wearing my red bandanna, everyone is afraid they be dead if they mess with me."

Many youths who join gangs come from backgrounds where there were no parental or adult advisors. The gang leader becomes the role model and the gang becomes a family to them. Gang membership offers adolescents status, acceptance, and self-esteem that they could not find at home or elsewhere. The breakdown of family and community structures can leave children more receptive to gang recruitment.

African Americans must never forget that, as a people, they "are the salt of the earth; but if the salt has lost its savor, wherewith shall it be salted? It is thenceforth good for nothing, but to be cast out, and to be trodden under foot of men" (Matthew 5:13). I believe that God made humans, and created the heavens and earth and all therein. African Americans, like any other group of people, were designed by God to be unique. Everyone God created, He created for a specific purpose, with skills and gifts that are different from those around them. African Americans, by acknowledging their history, will come to understand that they were created to be accurately and genetically perfect for solving many of the problems in their lives.

The truth of the matter is that African Americans are not just born to accomplish their own purpose, but to accomplish God's purpose. Self-knowledge is the beginning of identifying and accomplishing one's purpose. African Americans must recognize that their creation and birth is purpose-driven. When we discover who we are then we will discover the purpose for which we were created. It is only after this that we will begin to experience perfect peace, fulfillment, and provision for our own lives. It is not about a person's birthplace or color. Know that God made places before He made people; therefore, where you are is as important as what you are. Knowing and accepting one's history is integral to knowing who one is and what one should be about in life (Murdock, 1997). It is important that black people always remember their past while they are fighting for a brighter future.

CHAPTER TWO

Education

"Education, then, beyond other devices of human origin, is the great equalizer of the conditions of men— the balance-wheel of the social machinery."
—Benjamin Disraeli

The relevance of education to human development and welfare is beyond measure. Education opens the windows of opportunity to the comforts and luxuries that the world has to offer. I would like to point out that education is a phenomenon that starts from the day a person is born and continues until death. This means that education is not restricted to the bricks and mortar of a school complex; the world and happenings around us can and do educate us. There is no doubt that education provides a means by which the issues of poverty, race, class, and social inequalities can be dealt with in every society.

It has been said that ignorance is bliss and knowledge is power. An educated person is an open-minded person with self-confidence who will not hesitate to change his ways in order to improve his life. A person is no value to the working world without the proper kind of education. People's lives and the lives of their children will prosper in accordance with how much they are willing to educate themselves.

If all of the above are true about the importance of education, why are so many black Americans not encouraging educational excellence in their homes and communities? Why is the trend in black America today, "dumbing up" to be cool? Former President Lyndon Baines Johnson, on his declaration of war on poverty, stated that "Poverty has many roots, but the tap root is ignorance." Lack of access to the proper education is arguably one of the reasons why African Americans are one of the sub-communities that has not kept pace with the economic progress of the country as a whole; and in which many important respects, progress has been inhibited. The cliché that "knowledge is power" is so undeniably true, especially in the modern capitalistic society of the United States of America.

Lord Henry Brougham stated that "Education makes a people easy to lead, but difficult to drive; easy to govern, but difficult to enslave." This probably explains why African Americans were conditioned during slavery to cultivate a culture of dislike for education. African Americans came to the United States as slaves and to keep them enslaved the slave owners took every measure possible to keep them absolutely illiterate. As a matter of fact, there were laws established in this country during slavery that made it illegal to teach slaves how to read or write. Not only were there not many ways to learn these skills, but many slave masters would punish their slaves severely if they found out that they'd acquired the ability to read or write. In spite of these obstacles, some slaves still found ways to acquire literacy, but there weren't many places that could be called institutions for them to go to. Slaves were kept ignorant to the fact that there were ways in which they could be freed from slavery.

This sad revelation may help to explain why African Americans' education in America started out so rough. Since it was illegal to teach a slave to read and write during the time of slavery, many African Americans were completely illiterate at the time of emancipation.

Slave literacy and education

Initially, the United States saw blacks as inferior because they were uneducated and because they were also regarded as property. The constitution proclaimed that "all men are created equal," but this phrase excluded blacks from the equation. Many of the founding fathers of this nation were slave owners and some of the slave owners viewed blacks as intellectually inferior to whites, including Thomas Jefferson. All these barriers to blacks' access to education helped to perpetuate the view that blacks were ignorant and incapable of being educated citizens. This is not a justification for the denial of rights to blacks at that time but a view of how blacks were seen during the time of slavery (Mosley, 2009).

Black illiteracy was seen as key to maintaining slavery; the slaveholders considered keeping slaves ignorant a necessity to ensuring the security of the slaveholder. Slaves were banned from entering schoolhouses and could even be severely punished for so much as looking at a picture, depending on the whims of their owners. As a matter of fact, the desire of African Americans to learn how to read and write was very strong; that desire led to the *Nat Turner's Revolt* in Southampton County, Virginia during the summer of 1831.

Rev. John G. Fee, a native of Bracken County, Ky., believed in a school that would be an advocate of equality and excellence in education for men and women of all races. Fee's uncompromising faith and courage in preaching against slavery attracted the attention of Cassius M. Clay, a well-to-do Kentucky landowner and prominent leader in the movement for gradual emancipation. Clay felt he had found in Fee an individual who would take a strong stand on slavery. In 1853, Clay offered Fee a 10-acre homestead on the edge of the mountains if Fee would take up permanent residence there. Fee accepted and established an anti-slavery church with 13 members on a ridge they named "Berea" after the biblical town whose populace was open-minded and receptive to the gospel (Acts 17:10).

In 1855, a one-room school, that eventually would become Berea College, which also served as a church on Sundays, was built on a lot contributed by a neighbor. Berea's first teachers were recruited from Oberlin College, an anti-slavery stronghold in Ohio. Fee saw his humble church-school as the beginning of a sister institution "which would be to Kentucky what Oberlin is to Ohio, anti-slavery, anti-caste, anti-rum, anti-sin." A few months later, Fee wrote in a letter, "we...eventually look to a college – giving an education to all colors, classes, cheap and thorough."

Heather Andrea Williams, in tracing the historical antecedents to freed people's intense desire to become literate, demonstrates how the visions of enslaved African Americans emerged into plans and action once slavery ended. Enslaved people, Williams contends, placed great value in the practical power of literacy, whether it was to enable them to read the Bible for themselves or to stay informed of progress in the abolition movement or, later, the progress of the Civil War. She argues that by teaching, building schools, supporting teachers, resisting violence, and claiming education as a civil right, African Americans transformed the face of education in the South to the great benefit of both black and white southerners. It is important to point out that in the early part of the 19th century there were no schools in the southern states of America that admitted African American children to their free public schools systems. Some brave teachers, such as John Chavis in Raleigh, North Carolina, ran secret night schools. But teachers who were found educating African America children were run out of town. Margaret Douglass, who was caught teaching black children in Norfolk, Virginia, was convicted and imprisoned for her actions.

Williams' writings also reveal some of the early efforts of slaves and freedmen to educate themselves and their children. She points out that while freed people may have been motivated by the pecuniary benefits of education, they were also keenly aware that learning to read meant engaging in a monumental political movement. Her account covers the activities of many diverse groups, each playing their own particular role in a collective struggle: the clandestine efforts of slaves who broke anti-literacy laws in their efforts to read; the determination of ex-slaves-turned-Union-soldiers to learn to read in army camps, and to pass on that knowledge once they returned home; the demands of Reconstruction-era black politicians that education be provided to their children, so that they could enjoy the political privileges associated with citizenship; and the labor of students and teachers in the face of not only inadequate housing and textbooks, but also physical attacks and death threats from local whites.

She begins with a short history of slaves' attempts to get themselves educated in the antebellum South. These efforts were legally forbidden and thus such "perpetrators" were literally risking their life and limb in their determination to learn to read and write. While anti-literacy laws are generally thought of as a reaction to Nat Turner's 1831 rebellion, Williams revealed examples of such statutes a century before the uprising. Slave owners, it seems, were long wary that literacy would allow slaves to organize against their masters, and sought to limit their ability to communicate with one another. Blacks themselves were well aware of the connection between political power and literacy. One of the first groups of blacks to be exposed to any type of education were former slaves who fought in the Union Army, a group that would naturally be tapped for leadership positions after the war. Williams states that "African American soldiers were indeed anxious to become literate, as they stood to become leaders in their communities after the war. White soldiers were impressed by the common sight of their black comrades 'stand[ing] guard with book in hand.'"

Indeed, the first political leaders of post-war black communities prioritized education among the goals for which they would fight. One of the most interesting passages in Williams' writings describes the political conventions held by former slaves in southern states. Delegates met in order to draft demands to submit to all-white conventions charged with ratifying new, Reconstruction state constitutions. Although most demands were ignored, Williams writes: "Illiteracy, they knew, would impede their ambition for full participation in this public, political sphere. Therefore, alongside traditionally defined civil rights of suffrage and jury service, freed people propounded a new right: the right to attend school." Williams convincingly traces the rise of the common-school movement in the South to the efforts of former slaves to provide education to their children, and the resulting envy inspired in poor whites.

Williams even goes to great lengths to undermine an iconic image promoted in many history texts: that of the kindly Yankee schoolmarm benevolently descending upon ignorant ex-slaves. Instead, she presents a more nuanced picture of the pool of teachers in black schools. While she stresses that trained white teachers from the North were essential, she also highlights the role local blacks played. Using records kept by the Freedmen's Bureau itself {The Freedmen's Bureau, was a U.S. federal government agency that aided distressed freed slaves in 1865–1869, during the Reconstruction era of the United States}, she demonstrates that the majority of teachers in 1868 were black. Indeed, the estimated black share of teachers is probably a small number, as rural schools were both less likely to be counted in official records and more likely to be run by black teachers. Local black teachers were especially essential in these areas because the white "soldiers of light and love," as northern evangelicals were often called, were more comfortable in the Southern cities. Indeed, well over half of northern-born teachers, clergymen, and social workers living in the South in 1870 inhabited urban areas, whereas over ninety percent of blacks lived in rural areas. This spatial mismatch between the supply and demand of teachers was usually corrected by local black teachers.

Many black teachers were themselves once students of the typical Yankee schoolmarms. The positive ripple effects of education are another key theme in Williams' book. As soon as a student became literate, he became a teacher himself, either officially or unofficially, by passing on what he learned to his family and friends. "Education was not a commodity to be selfishly hoarded," she writes. "Rather, many freed people considered it an asset that should be spread around the community. The positive spillovers of literacy from children to parents appear to be the most important route by which adults learned to read in the decade after the war. While more than ten percent of southern blacks between the ages of ten and fourteen attended school in 1870, less than one half of one percent of Southern blacks over twenty-five did so. Williams is less clear on this point: at times she describes parents attending school alongside their children, yet in other places notes that parents rarely attended classes.

Another point on which Williams could be no clearer is the role of black churches in early education. Williams describes the efforts of Northern groups such as the American Missionary Association (AMA)— including very revealing accounts of the AMA's battles with local freedmen over control of black schools—but gives far less attention to local religious institutions. She notes that "[m]any southern towns had at least two black churches, one Methodist and one Baptist, that were both transformed into classrooms for adults and children on weekdays and on Sundays they housed Sabbath schools." But this only begs the question of the antebellum status of these black churches; had they been independently run by free Southern blacks? Or had they been established by whites in order to appease their slaves? Similarly, Williams writes that black ministers often emerged as community leaders in the early days of emancipation because they were more likely to be literate, but she never describes what these men did in the slave communities before the war (Williams, 2005).

Post-emancipation literacy and education

Slavery finally ended in the United States after the Civil War, and it was now okay for African Americans to be educated. But access to quality education for African Americans was still not available in the United States. Booker T. Washington, born as a slave in Hale's Ford, Virginia, believed that the most effective means by which African Americans could make the transition from slavery to full emancipation was through economic development. He saw a direct relationship between education and economic development; hence, in 1881 he founded the Tuskegee Normal and Industrial Institute, today known as Tuskegee University. This school taught agricultural science and industrial skills with the intention of preparing students to become profitable landowners and entrepreneurs. With access to education and a growing hunger for it, a tide of generations of political and economic advocacy started to grow in the African American communities. African Americans sought education even though they may not have access to a formal institution of education (Andrews, 2001).

As early as 1849, African Americans filed suit against an educational system that mandated racial segregation, in the case of *Roberts v. City of Boston.* The United States Supreme Court's 1954 decision in *Oliver Brown et al. v. the Board of Education of Topeka (KS) et al.* dismantled the legal basis for racial segregation in schools and other public facilities. This case, among other significant court cases, was a turning point in the educational development of the United States. Many of these cases struck down the existing segregated educational system as a product supporting the human tendencies to prejudge, discriminate against, and stereotype people by their ethnic, religious, physical, or cultural characteristics.

Literacy and education in the 21st Century

Let me begin by saying that the truth about how most blacks perceive education today has been a hard pill for blacks to swallow. Many African Americans seem to believe that the "natural" order of the economy leaves them always at the bottom and there is little prospect of a just reward for being educated. This may explain why, throughout our recent history, education seems to be at the very bottom of black America's priorities. Blacks have become part of the American "underclass" because their lack of skills or high-quality schooling has rendered them largely unemployable in the legal economy. The shift in the composition of jobs toward technical and highly educated workers means that poorly schooled people face bleak job prospects, without much ability to move from the weak to the more prosperous sectors of the labor market.

Furthermore, the most fundamental findings of social scientists who study education reveal that the best predictor of the educational achievements of children is the level of education attained by their parents. Going to school creates a "taste" for school that is then passed on to future generations. Neighborhoods with high concentrations of poor and unemployed people tend to be places with high crime rates, low levels of academic achievement, high rates of divorce, and high rates of teenage childbearing. Even working-class blacks are muddling through an economy that no longer offers the prospect of middle-class life to hardworking but modestly educated adults (Andrews, 2001).

Now, let us for a brief moment, take a look at the way some right-wing fundamentalists explain how the African American attitude toward education has contributed to their poverty. Richard Herrnstein and Charles Murray, in their book *The Bell Curve,* present three central explanations for black poverty: (1) Most of our nation's social problems, from income inequality across class and color lines to crime, reflect basic differences in the intellectual abilities of people to cope with the complex task associated with life in a modern society. (2) Intellectual differences between successful and unsuccessful people are primarily, though not exclusively, due to genetically-based differences in raw cognitive capacities that can be accurately measured by various types of IQ tests. (3) Raw cognitive abilities are passed across the generations through families, with the result that social hierarchies are reproduced over time because low IQ parents tend to bear low IQ children. Their position is that if African Americans would only accept their fate as less intelligent, and therefore less well-off members of the American nation, then most racial problems would disappear, leaving society with the profound but ultimately nonracial question of how to care for our poorer and less intelligent members of society (Herrnstein & Murray, 1996).

Dinesh D'Souza, in his book *The End of Racism,* offers some basic explanations for how black attitude toward education has contributed to black poverty: (1) He states that blacks are, on the average, poorer than whites because blacks have failed to acquire the appropriate forms and levels of education and technical knowledge. (2) Blacks exhibit low levels of intellectual and academic achievements compared to whites, Asians and Hispanics. These low levels of academic achievement are the main reason for the relatively poor performance of blacks in the job market and in all areas of endeavor tied to intellectual achievement. (3)The primary reason for low levels of black intellectual and academic achievement is not that blacks are an intellectually inferior subspecies by virtue of their genetic inheritance, but that the cultural inheritance of African Americans cripples them in highly competitive academic and economic systems.

He writes that "African Americans are burdened by a maladaptive oppositional culture that views learning, intellectual achievement, delayed gratification, sexual restraint (especially among the young), marriage, and abhorrence of violence as signs of capitulation to an oppressive white system." His position is that African Americans who complain of "racism" in the post-civil rights era are making excuses for avoiding the hard work of competing in the open arenas of a free market and modern schools. He claims that African Americans are the victims of their bad culture which promotes bad behavior and values, and that if they stop being so silly and adopt more civilized ways of living, then they will be respectable and acceptable to the rest of the society. This, he claims, will be when racism will end (D'Souza, 1995). Herrnstein, Murray and D'Souza see a link between race and economic backwardness. They seem to subscribe to the idea that black people are either dumb by nature, or are made stupid by culture. They are therefore implying that something is wrong with black people for them not to seek education now that they have access to high quality education.

Dr. William Henry Cosby, bluntly speaking about African American behavior toward education in a gala at Constitution Hall in Washington DC, says: "They're standing on the corner and they can't speak English. I can't even talk the way these people talk:

> "Why you ain't,
> Where you is,
> What he drive,
> Where he stay,
> Where he work,
> Who you be. . . ."

He goes on to say,

And I blamed the kid until I heard the mother talk. And then I heard the father talk. Everybody knows it's important to speak English except these knuckleheads. You can't be a doctor with that kind of crap coming out of your mouth. In fact you will never get any kind of job making a decent living. People marched and were hit in the face with rocks to get an education, and now we've got these knuckleheads walking around. The lower economic people are not holding up their end in this deal. These people are not parenting. They are buying things for kids. $500 sneakers for what? And they won't spend $200 for "Hooked on Phonics. I am talking about these people who cry when their son is standing there in an orange suit. Where were you when he was two? Where were you when he was twelve? Where were you when he was eighteen and how come you didn't know that he had a pistol? And where is the father? Or who is his father? People putting their clothes on backward. Isn't that a sign of something gone wrong? People with their hats on backward, pants down around the crack, isn't that a sign of something? Isn't it a sign of something when she has her dress all the way up and got all type of needles [piercings] going through her body? What part of Africa did this come from? Today a woman has eight children with eight different 'husbands'—or men or whatever you call them now. We have millionaire football players who cannot read. We have million-dollar basketball players who can't write two paragraphs. We, as black folks, have to do a better job. Someone working at Wal-Mart with seven kids, you are hurting us. We have to start holding each other to a higher standard" (Cosby, 2004).

His argument, as I see it, is that African Americans, with the educational opportunities that are now available to them, can no longer blame whites for their own economic demise.

There was uproar in the African American community when Cosby made those comments. But if the truth be told, if you take a good look at the African American family structure, you will find that there is validity to his perception of the root of the problems for the African American family. Malcolm X said that "education is our passport to the future, for tomorrow belongs to those who prepare for it today." I believe that Dr. Cosby's frustration comes from the culture of the lack of interest in education that pervades the African American communities today.

African Americans now have access to high quality education. The questions they must now address are; why do African Americans today no longer take education as seriously as their slave ancestors? Why do blacks now see education as a joke? Why do many African American parents no longer have an interest in the education of their children? Why has it become so hard to get African American parents to attend Parent-Teacher Association (PTA) or Parent-Teacher Organization (PTO) meetings, School Board meetings, open houses at their children's schools, and even parents-teacher conferences? Why is it so rare to find African American parents volunteering at their kids' schools? Why do increasing numbers of African American parents now use schools as babysitting centers? Why do many blacks now look at education as a "white thing" and the pursuit of it as an attempt to act "white" and as such be tantamount to "selling out"? How do blacks explain why their kids now "dumb up" to be "cool"? Why do African American parents allow their children to rise to low expectation?

Furthermore, unlike their predecessors, too many African American teachers, especially those in predominantly African American schools, now think about only the monetary rewards from teaching; they seem to lack the joyful feeling of satisfaction that comes from being a teacher. Most of them no longer care about teaching as their way of contributing to the future of their pupils; they see their teaching jobs only as a source of "bread and butter." Some black teachers in these predominantly black K-12 public schools are quick to call their students out of their names; they refer to them as riff raffs, hoodlums, thugs, et cetera. They are very reluctant to take the time and patience to work with their students. Some of these teachers act as if taking the time to teach these students is doing the students a favor, rather than performing the duties for which they were hired.

Also, many African American parents today have no respect for the educational environment. When some of these parents are invited to schools (K-12) for conferences about their children, if they come at all, they would rather pick a fight with the school authority and not discuss the problem at hand and find solutions to the problems their children are having in school. This reminds me of what I observed in a middle school in the Tallahassee, Florida area. On this day, I was in the reception area waiting to visit with one of my young advisees, when a parent came bursting into the office entrance asking for her child's teacher. She was not just loud but she was using profanity. Let me also mention that this parent came to the school at about 10:15 am, with rollers on her head and wearing house shoes and a pair of pants that looked like pajamas. It was apparent that she had not come to the school to discuss with the school authorities why her child had been suspended for three days.

Hearing her ranting, it was obvious that she was more concerned with how this child being at home was going to obstruct her peace and quiet. She demanded to see the teacher, yelling, "I want to see that teacher, that bitch who suspended my child so I can whup their ass." All of these, by the way, were happening in the presence of her child and other children who had come to the front office for several other reasons. And what about those parents who keep their children home from school so they, their children, and their children's friends can get high on drugs, get drunk, or just have a party?

An African proverb states that "it takes a village to raise a child." This proverb is more relevant today in the need for the village's participation in the education of African American children than ever before. But the involvement of the village today is almost entirely restricted to sporting events. It is almost impossible to get African American parents or adults to attend PTA/ PTO meetings or parent-teacher conferences. It is sometimes very hard for a school to get in touch with a parent or an adult family member of a child at all. But when it comes to sporting events, the sporting facility will be packed with parents, aunties, uncles, grandparents, cousins, and godparents—no matter what the time of the day may be—for little Johnnie's or Teniqua's game. I always wonder: if this many people are interested in these children's sporting events, where are they when it comes to the children's education issues? In too many black homes is the path out of poverty seen to be through athletics and entertainment not education. This probably explains why most African American families expose their children to and invest their resources on athletics and entertainment.

Our problem is that too many of us see sports as the way out of our socioeconomic slump. Reports show that there are actually a number of African Americans who have been fortunate to work professionally in sports or entertainment, but because they lack the proper education they end up becoming poor after their professional career. Because they lacked the knowledge of good financial planning and management, they were unable to monitor their bank accounts.

There is no doubt that parents' involvement at home in their children's education improves students' performance in school. Not only does their involvement contribute to their children going further in education, but it will also improve the quality of education provided by the school. When parents are involved at school as well as at home, children do better and stay in school longer. The family makes critical contributions to student achievement from preschool through high school. When children and parents talk regularly about school, children perform better academically. (Aston & McLanahan, 1991; Finn, 1993). A home environment that encourages learning is more important to student achievement than income, education level, or cultural background. (Henderson and Berla, 1994).

Harold D. Wright (2010) proclaimed that:

"When test scores from the school district which I live are examined, black students have the worst scores. The lowest performing schools in the district are those schools with predominantly black student population. Now, there are many reasons for this academic phenomenon in this country and probably elsewhere. One thing is certain, white students are not naturally more intelligent or gifted than black students. One major reason this achievement gap exists is attitude. Many of us have seen the poster with the statement 'Your attitude determines your altitude'".

As a race, black adults should challenge their children to be the smartest in the class. It very common to hear black kids saying, 'I don't want to be the smartest in my class. People will think I am a geek or dork'. Does I am not claiming that this attitude permeate the thinking of most black students. However, it is certainly now the attitude of far too many black students. If our children continue to believe that being smart is acting white, we are doomed as a people.... It is disappointing when students frown upon learning at any time. But the attitude toward school and learning starts in the home. Parents must create a learning environment in the home. It is the parent, first and foremost, who must encourage and reward their children for academic achievement.

Black students continue to have too many athletes and entertainers placed before them as examples of success and as role models. Parents must set high academic expectations for their children such that average is not acceptable and failure must not be tolerated. We are the rescuers we have been waiting for. Right now, the white man can rid himself of guilt by giving our children books that they won't read. He doesn't fear change in the status quo as long as too many of our children think intelligence is not natural to them.

We must teach our black children their history, which demonstrates clearly our intellectual achievement. We must show our children what blacks are achieving today due to academic success. Most importantly, each and every one of us and parents in particular must be an example. If we continue to put the emphasis on the physical and not mental, we have no one to blame but ourselves. Being smart is acting like the Africans who introduced civilization to the world. It is acting like the Africans who invented paper, medicine, chemistry and who built pyramids. Africans set the standards for intellectual achievement in the world and we must continue to do so."

CHAPTER THREE

Spending to Impress Others

"I was part of that strange race of people aptly described as spending their lives doing things they detest, to make money they don't want, to buy things they don't need, to impress people they dislike."
—Emile Henry Gauvreau

Do the clothes a person wears, the vehicle one drives, the places one shops, and the restaurants one dines at determine a person's status in society? In other words, is what a person acquires and owns a reflection of the person's personal identity? Research shows that a majority of millionaires live a frugal lifestyle—searching for bargains, purchasing used automobiles, and shopping at discount stores like Wal-Mart, JC Penney, Ross, Family Dollar and even Goodwill Stores.

Why do so many African Americans think that their outward appearance defines who they are? Too many blacks buy things to camouflage or fool others of who they truly are. We spend to present an attractive image of ourselves. If we take a look at the black community, it is obvious that more and more blacks are subscribing to this practice of pretentious spending. Black people just want to be "super fly."

There is no doubt that higher rates of unemployment, income disparity between blacks and whites, and credit discrimination are some of the key factors that inhibit economic vitality of blacks. However, we must acknowledge that consumers' spending habits may be the greatest financial impediment to our economic vitality. Blacks earn approximately $631 billion annually, and if we can change our spending habits we will be able to reduce our economic hardship substantially.

Nationwide data on consumption reveals that blacks and Hispanics devote large shares of their expenditure to visible goods (clothing, jewelry, and cars) than do whites at comparable income levels. While racial differences in satisfaction preference parameters might account for a portion of these consumption differences, research reveals a large body of anecdotal evidence suggesting that blacks devote a larger share of their overall expenditure to consumption items that are readily visible to the outside observers than do whites (Charles et al, 2007).

An article in AmericanRenaissance.Com entitled *Black Spending Habits* states that according to Target Market, a company that tracks black consumer spending,

African Americans spend a significant amount of their income on depreciable products. In 2002, the year that the U.S. economy started its nose-dive, blacks spent $22.9 billion on clothes, $3.2 billion on electronics, and $11.6 billion on furniture for their homes that, in most cases, were rental homes. Among their favorite purchases are cars and liquor. Blacks make up only 12% of the US population, yet:

- They account for 30% of the country's Scotch consumption.
- Detroit, which is 80% African American, is the world's number one market for Cognac.
- African Americans spend over 75% more than whites on boys' clothes.
- African Americans are estimated to spend more than $500 million per year on McDonald's fast food,
- African Americans consume 32% of all malt liquor products.
- African Americans males between the ages of 13 and 24, who are less than 3% of the total U.S. population, account for 10% of the $12 billion athletic shoe market, purchasing more that 1 out of 5 pairs of shoes made by Nike.
- African American females, who make up about 6% of the total U.S. population, purchase 15% of the $4 billion cosmetics industry, or $600 million, and spend 26% more on perfume than any other group of females.

- The report states that Lincoln Automaker was so impressed with the $46.7 billion that blacks spent on cars that the automaker commissioned Sean "P Diddy" Comb, the entertainer and fashion mogul, to design a limited-edition Navigator replete with six plasma screens, three DVD players, and a Sony PlayStation 2.

The tracking revealed that the only area where African Americans seem to be cutting back on spending is books; total purchases have gone down from a high of $356 million in 2000 to $303 million in 2002. This shortsighted behavior, the Target report pointed out, must be motivated by a desire for instant gratification and social acceptance—to the detriment of future economic development.

According to the published report, the Ariel Mutual Funds/Charles Schwab *2003 Black Investor Survey* found that when comparing black and white households of similar incomes, whites saved nearly 20% more each month for retirement. Additionally, 30% of African Americans earning $100,000 a year had less than $5,000 in retirement savings. While 79% of whites invest in the stock market, only 61% of African Americans do (AmericanRenaissance.Com, 2006). The National Urban League's 2004 *The State of Black America* report found that fewer than 50% of black families owned their homes compared to more than 70% of whites.

What about life insurance? It is common in the African American community to see family members soliciting for funds to pay for the burial of their deceased relative who had neither life insurance nor savings to pay for their own funeral. In a good number of these cases, the individual may have "lived large" when they were alive: driving the nicest cars, living in big houses, wearing designer clothes, going on expensive vacations, and never missed travelling to their favorite black college's football classic played anywhere in the country. Too many black people die leaving no inheritance to their surviving family members. Instead, they leave them with a lot of debts—they lived to impress other and spent far beyond their means.

In 2001, I received a forwarded email, supposedly written by one Derrick E. Price, a Caucasian. Some of you may have also seen it. I am not sure of its authenticity, but it is so relevant to this topic that I've decided to include it as a narrative in this chapter. This email is entitled "They Are Still Our Slaves." It starts with,

"We continue to reap profits from the blacks without the efforts of physical slavery. Look at the current methods of containment that they use on themselves: IGNORANCE, GREED, and SELFISHNESS.

Their IGNORANCE is the primary weapon of containment. A great man once said, "The best way to hide something from black people is to put it in a book." We live now in the information age. They have gained the opportunity to read any

book on any subject through the efforts
of their fight for freedom, yet they refuse
to read. There are numerous books readily available at Borders, Barnes & Noble,
and Amazon.com, not to mention their
own black Bookstores that provide solid
blueprints to reach economic equality; but
few read consistently, if they read at all.

GREED is another powerful weapon
of containment. Blacks, since the abolition of slavery, have had large amounts
of money at their disposal. Last year
they spent over $10 billion dollars dur-
ing Christmas, out of their $450 billion
in total yearly income. Any one of us can
use them as our target market—for any
business venture we care to dream up, no
matter how outlandish, they will buy into
it. Being primarily a consumer people,
they function totally by greed. They con-
tinually want more, with little thoughts
of saving or investing. They would rather
buy some new sneaker than invest in
starting a business. Some of them neglect
their children to have the latest Tommy
or FUBU. And they still think that having a Cadillac, Mercedes, or multiple cars
give them "status" or means they have
achieved the American Dream. They are
fools!

The vast majority of their people are still in poverty because their greed holds them back from collectively making better communities for themselves. With the help of BET [Black Entertainment Television] and the rest of their black media that often broadcasts destructive images into their own homes, we will continue to see huge profits like those in Tommy and Nike. Tommy Hilfiger has even jeered them by saying he doesn't want their money, but look at how the fools still spend more with him than before.

SELFISHNESS, a culture ingrained in their minds during slavery, is one of the major ways we can continue to contain them. One of their own, W.E.B. Dubois said that there was an innate division in their culture, a "Talented Tenth" he called it. He was correct in his deduction that there is a segment of their population that has achieved some "form" of success. However, that segment missed the fullness of his work. They didn't read that the "Talented Tenth" was responsible to aid the "Non-Talented Ninety Percent in achieving a better life. Instead, that segment has created another class, a "Buppie" class that looks at their people or aids them in a condescending manner. They will never achieve what we have.

Their selfishness does not allow them to be able to work together on any project or endeavor of substance. When they get together, their selfishness lets their ego get in the way of the goal. Their so-called help organizations seem to only want to promote their names without making any real change in their communities. They are content to sit in conferences and conventions in our hotels and talk about what they will do, while they award plaques to the best speakers, not the best doers.

Is there no end to their selfishness? They steadfastly refuse to see that "Together Each Achieves More" (TEAM!). They do not understand that they are no better than each other because of what they own. The unfortunate fact is that most of those "Buppies" are but one pay check from poverty. All of which is under the control of our pens in our offices and boardrooms."

There is no doubt in my mind that the American Dream has to do with the accumulation of wealth and financial independence. Why then do African Americans still tend to spend much of their money on some of the most depreciable items? Why do some of us still subscribe to a culture of pretentious consumption? Some people may argue that this issue of consumerism is an epidemic that is seeping through all of America, but I am here to declare that like all other diseases, it disproportionately affects the African American community.

It is common, when driving through densely populated African American neighborhoods, to see frivolous spending like a 1996 Chevrolet Caprice fitted with $5,500 24-inch chromed rims and painted in a $7,500 marble paint job. And, in some cases, the stereo/DVD system and the multiple TV monitors in that car may be worth every bit of $18,000. Some of these cars have customized upholstery with monogrammed seat covers costing at least $15,000.

The saddest part of the story is that most of the owners of these vehicles either live with some woman or friend and they don't have a place of their own to live. There are occasions when one might even see multiple late model luxury vehicles, belonging to one person or a family of two who live in a rented apartment or a government subsidized housing unit. There are young black men who own twenty to thirty New Era caps and twenty pairs of Air Force One shoes, with no plans for the future but to buy some more caps and shoes and rap about them. There are some blacks who may have been fortunate to have access to some money, and have no problem paying $50 to $150 for club admissions or $500 to $1,500 for a reserved table at someone else's club to drink overpriced drinks, just to impress others. Sometimes, some of these people even engage in the practice of "making it rain" in the club. This is a practice where a person comes up on stage with a pile of money in hand and then begins to toss it into the crowd a handful at a time.

African Americans seem to have spending pathologies that reflect a deeply programmed sense of pretentious spending. A large majority of us do judge the book by its cover; a psychosis of materialism. Some people may argue that blacks, being the only group of people in this country that were ever subjected to the degrading chattel of America's slavery, adopted a materialistic attitude to compensate for their lack of self-esteem.

As a matter of fact, too many blacks spend too much of the money they don't have, to buy things they don't need, trying to impress people they don't even like and probably don't even care about. This reminds me of a situation that took place in 2000, during my tenure as the President of the Tallahassee, Florida Branch of the National Association for the Advancement of Colored People (NAACP). A young black lady called the office to complain about a situation she deemed racially discriminatory. Her complaint was that she and her five kids were evicted by her white landlord for no reason, and she wanted the NAACP to come to her rescue. We scheduled an appointment for her to come by the office so she could complete an official complaint form, which would give the NAACP the authority to investigate her complaint on her behalf.

On the day of the scheduled meeting, she arrived about forty-five minutes late with all of her five kids. I must admit that she and all of her kids were looking good. Every strand of her hair was in its proper place, and her fingers and toe nails looked professionally manicured and pedicured respectively with decorative rhinestones. Her children were neatly dressed in Tommy Hilfiger, Calvin Klein, and FUBU outfits and Reeboks and Nike shoes. She had on one of the largest sets of gold earrings I have ever seen on a woman and other jewelry to match.

By the way, she was brought to the office by another young lady who was also very nicely dressed. Now, here is where the story changes. Upon completing the complaint form I joined her for the interview to hear what her situation was all about. She told me that she came home one afternoon, after spending the previous night at her girlfriend's place, to find her belongings outside her apartment, on the curbside of the road. Although she admitted that she hadn't been able to pay her rent for some time, she thought the actions of her landlord— a white male—were because she was black, and that this was unfair and unjust. She insisted that her landlord didn't care about the fact that she had five kids and was pregnant with another.

At this point in the conversation, I decided to take a peek at the complaint form to see how old she really was. She was almost twenty-six years old. Her situation demonstrates the way that many blacks suffer because they have cultivated an attitude of spending to impress others. Here she was, a twenty-five year old, unemployed, with five children and expecting a sixth child. Rather than using whatever money she received from whatever sources, to pay her rent to ensure having a shelter over her and her children's head, she decided to spend her money on clothes and things that enhanced her and her children's outward appearance. I would like to point out at this juncture that she was on the Housing and Urban Development (HUD) program. Although her total rent was $1,075 monthly, she was required to pay only $65. It was the $65 monthly out-of-pocket payment that she was claiming to be too much for her to handle. Of course, you know we told her there was nothing the NAACP could do for her in that case. However, we referred her to some other social services organizations to see if they could provide her the assistance she needed. She wasn't happy and left the office with a few choice words that were not flattering about the NAACP.

I don't know how many people really pay any attention to parents on Aid for Families with Dependent Children (AFDC) during the tax season. Some of these parents who are unemployed but have multiple children get approximately twelve thousand dollars in refunds. Many of these parents spend all of this money on everything except the upkeep and education of their children. I just happened to be in an elementary school in Gadsden County, Florida one day, when a parent was called to the school to talk about one of her children attending that school.

I noticed that this child had on oversized pants with no belt, and as a result he had to hold the waist of these pants balled up in one hand. It was brought to my attention that this young man was one of the smartest pupils in the school. But the issue here was that the mother had refused to purchase this child a belt even though he had been a subject of ridicule by other children. The child's mother was called to the school because the situation surrounding the pants was beginning to adversely impact his self-image and consequently his desire for social participation and academic performance.

I overheard the mother say, "I ain't buying no damn belt for that boy because I ain't got no money for shit like that." But on her way out of the office she bumped into a custodian she knew and they started to talk, and loudly. In that conversation, I overheard her telling this custodian, in a bragging way, that she had just received her income tax check of over ten thousand dollars and was about to travel to Miami to shop and have her some fun. Now, what is wrong with this picture? Here is the parent of a very smart kid who doesn't see the importance of investing in his future, even though the income tax refund she received was earned income credit for the children she had. The ridicules that this very smart child is being subjected to at such a young age may cause him to lose interest in school and take a path of deviant behavior that could lead him to a life of poverty or crime when he gets older. This mother, like many others, would rather spend any money that comes her way on things she thinks will make her look good in her outward appearance, rather than on things that may change her life and that of her children for the better.

A few years ago there was a very intelligent young man in one of my economics classes at Florida A&M

University in Tallahassee, Florida. This young man was smart and I just knew that he was destined for greatness. But before the semester ended, his uncle passed and left him with a sizeable inheritance—at least, that was what he told me. He suddenly stopped coming to my class, and I asked the class if anyone had heard from him or had any idea of what was going on with him. At a later time, when I asked the class again, a student told me that he had decided to drop out of school.

One day, I just happened to run into him at a grocery store, all dressed up like someone with some money. I'd also like to mention that he had two very gorgeous, with emphasis on the gorgeous, ladies hanging all over him. After I complimented him on how nice he looked I asked him about school. His response was that school was not for him anymore since the main purpose of going to school was to be able to find a decent paying job anyway. "Now I have the money," he said. "There's no need to waste my time with school anymore." I attempted to convince him about the importance of education, but he was adamant on his position regarding the irrelevance of education in his life.

When I finished my shopping I waited for him to complete his shopping so I could talk with him some more. We left the grocery store together and I continued my attempt to get him to understand the importance of education. I told him about learning how to invest and manage his inheritance so that he could be guaranteed a comfortable living for a very long time. But he still wouldn't even consider any of what I had to say.

All he wanted to talk about was what he was wearing, and how all his clothes were designer and/or custom and tailor made suits and shirts. He took the time to show me his gold cufflinks and the 18K gold Rolex watch that he had on.

As we were walking and talking, we walked toward a black car, which I came to learn, was a Bentley. This car was "smooth," as the kids would say; it had all the bells and whistles I could only imagine in a car. I again complimented him on his nice car. When we got closer to the car, he remotely started it, opened the doors, and asked the ladies to go on and get in so he could continue his conversation with his teacher. We talked for a little more but I was not successful at getting his attention in the direction I was trying to lead him. I became convinced that he was taking time to talk with me out of respect and I told him how much I truly appreciated that.

Four years later, I saw his photo flashed on the local evening news, as a suspect in an armed robbery. The story was that he went into one of the local banks with a handgun, demanding money from the clerk. He got some money and was able to get away but his picture was captured on the surveillance camera. Since he was very flashy in his lifestyle, it didn't take long for law enforcement to catch up with him and arrest him. He is presently serving life in prison for committing a crime in Florida with a handgun (State of Florida 10-20-Life Law). All of his spending was to impress others and to present an image that he thought represented success.

My only explanation for his decision to go rob a bank is that he probably exhausted his inheritance and still wanted to live the lifestyle he had become accustomed to since he received the inheritance. Smart spending is not only self-empowering, it is also community empowering. So, let's become smart spenders.

An unknown author writes:

"According to research by Kerwin Kofi Charles, Erik Hurst and Nikolai Roussanov, *Conspicuous Consumption and Race,* conspicuous consumption serves less to establish the owner's positive status as affluent than to fend off the negative perception that the owner is poor. The richer a society or peer group, the less important visible spending becomes". The writer states that "The researchers hypothesized that visible consumption lets individuals show strangers they aren't poor. Since strangers tend to lump people together by race, the lower your racial group's income, the more valuable it is to demonstrate your personal buying power" (Progressdaily.Com, 2008).

Many of the most successful people in the world have a few common values that they subscribe to, and if blacks can follow their lead, they too can make it big. Warren Buffett, who is worth $45 billion, still lives in the same Omaha, Nebraska, home he bought in 1958 for $31,500. If black people follow his frugal formula, they too may wind up with a lot more money than they ever dreamed.

On October 5, 2010, Yahoo's *Financially Fit* site provided five tips to build wealth and success:

1. Live Below Your Means.

Being wealthy isn't just a product of your salary or investment prowess; it's learning how to save. "We can make a lot of money, you can make a little bit of money, but the second you spend all the money is when people get into trouble. Saving is the key to preserving your wealth," says Ed Butowsky, managing partner of Chapwood Capital Investment Management, a firm that manages money for wealthy individuals.

As many Americans realized during the booming real estate market, just because you think you can afford something doesn't mean you should buy it. Keeping an eye on your bottom line will pay dividends over the long term.

2. Bounce Back From Defeat

With nearly fifteen million workers unemployed right now in the U.S., it's easy to get discouraged. Don't! Most successful and wealthy people have overcome obstacles and failure along the way. Steve Jobs

was ousted from Apple when he was thirty.
Today, he's a billionaire and a legend.
Plus, after getting fired, he created another
billion-dollar media company, Pixar.

"Bouncing back from defeat is something all great achievers have. They have
this undying belief good things will happen and will continue to happen," says
Butowsky.

Take Michael Jordan. "His Airness"
was cut from his high school basketball
team. Motivated by the rejection, Jordan
became a star the next season. The rest is
history.

3. Self-Promote

Regardless of the profession, the rich
and successful tend to have a strong sense
of self-worth—key to skillfully navigating
an upward career path. Mark Hurd, who
was ousted as CEO of Hewlett-Packard in
August, couldn't be kept down for long.
Using his business skills and connections,
in September, Hurd was named president
of Oracle. (Hurd and Oracle founder Larry
Ellison are known to be close friends.)

4. Have Street Smarts

Bernie Madoff lived the high life for
decades, scamming unsuspecting clients,

with a money-making formula that proved too good to be true. Only afterward did we learn that with a little due diligence, most clients could have easily uncovered the fraud.

But it's not only the swindlers and the con men you have to watch out for. Many times, friends and family take advantage of the rich. Whether it's a handout or an investment idea, Butowsky advises his high net worth clients that in most cases, it's wisest to just say "no." The best way to do that: have someone else do it for you.

"You need to really set up a wall between you and your family," he advises. "If you don't want to give them (family or friends) money . . . saying no is probably a good idea."

5. Buy Cheap

The rich can afford to splurge, but that doesn't mean they do. On New York City's Upper East Side, Michael's—The Consignment Shop for Women—has been a bargain-hunting destination for more than 60 years. "We have a good percentage of women who can afford to shop on Madison Avenue but really like the idea

of saving that money," says proprietor
Tammy Gates.

From Chanel to Gucci and Louis
Vuitton, the store specializes in high-
end designer merchandise for a reasonable price. Speaking of her clientele,
Gates says, "they're wealthy for a reason.
They recognize that bargains keep people
wealthy. Paying top dollar when you don't
have to doesn't make sense" (Gorenstein
and Torabi, 2010).

CHAPTER FOUR

The Blame Game

*"Responsible people do not blame circumstances,
conditions, or conditioning for their behavior. Their
behavior is a product of their own conscious choice."*
—Stephen Covey

There is a saying in my native Nigerian language which translates, states that "when one points a finger at the world or some other person, one must remember that three fingers are being pointed at oneself." A study published in *The Journal of Experimental Social Psychology* concluded that blame can be contagious. This study also revealed that pointing a finger at others is a way a person attempts to protect his or her own self-image. It seems natural for humans to play this game. When people blame others for their mistakes, they learn less and perform worse. This problem is magnified when blame becomes embedded in the shared culture of groups and organizations (Fast and Tiedens, 2010).

The bible tells a story, in Genesis 3:12, that when God confronted Adam after he had eaten the forbidden fruit in spite of the fact that he was specifically asked not to get close to it, Adam blamed Eve for giving it to him. He did not own up to nor take responsibility for his own actions.

People play the blame game because it gives them a false sense of gratification to say that someone or something else is responsible for their unhappy situation. Moreover, admitting our being responsible for our own unhappiness can be very scary. Many black people have become masters of the blame game. We live in a culture of blame and have adopted the seductive elements of the blame game; it has become too many black people's way of life. Erika Duffy stated that "we (people) always tend to stay in familiar patterns because we get comfortable there. Negative patterns can repeat themselves and unfortunately very severe issues can be passed down from generation to generation" (Duffy, 2010).

Black people blame white people who enslaved them, the color of their own skin, government policies, their families, and everyone and everything else for their state of poverty and failures in life. "The problem with the blame game is that it takes the attention and focus away from where it should be. We need to move beyond the 'it's not my fault' victim mentality and imbibe the humility, grace, and courage to do what it takes to accomplish change, progress, and success. As long as we think of ourselves as victims, we remain so and accomplish little or nothing." (Bridges, 2010).

Pastor O. Jermaine Simmons in his July 31, 2011
sermon at Jacob Chapel Baptist Church in Tallahassee,
Florida said:

"I'm reminded of an old adage which
was spoken by Fredrick Douglas that simply says "If there is no struggle there is
no progress. This struggle may be a moral
one, or it may be a physical one, and it
may be both moral and physical, but it
must be a struggle. Men may not get all
they pay for in this world; but they must
certainly pay for all they get. If we ever
get free from the oppressions and wrongs
heaped upon us, we must pay for their
removal. We must do this by labor, by
suffering, by sacrifice, and if needs be,
by our lives and the lives of others." This
prolific and prophetic statement was one
of the more memorable lines from his
speech *The Significance of Emancipation
in the West Indies* which he delivered in
Canandaigua, New York on August 3,
1857. The bulk of his dissertation was
predicated on the fight for British emancipation, and how West Indies slaves played
a huge part in that struggle for freedom…

Listen if you please. I hear Douglas
telling us that the general sentiment of
mankind is that a man, who will not fight
for himself, when he has the means of

81

doing so, is not worth being fought for by others. For a man who does not value freedom for himself, will never value it for others, or put himself to any inconvenience to gain it for others... Such a man, the world says, may lie down until he has sense enough to stand up. It is useless and cruel to put a man on his legs, if the next moment his head is to be brought against a curbstone. Yeah, a man of that type, will never lay the world under any obligation to him, but (rather) will be a moral pauper, a drag on the wheels of society, and if he too be identified with a peculiar variety of the race, he will entail disgrace upon his race as well as upon himself... I understand Douglas as letting us know that the world in which we live is very accommodating to all sorts of people. In other words, it will cooperate with them in any measure which they propose. It will help those who earnestly help themselves, and will hinder those who hinder themselves. It is very polite, and never offers its services unasked. Its favors to individuals are measured by an unerring principle (which is) to respect those who respect themselves, and despise those who despise themselves.

I hear him saying that it is not within the power of unaided human nature, to persevere in pitying a people who are insensible to their own wrongs and indifferent to the attainment of their own rights. The poet was as true to common sense as to poetry when he said, "(Whoever) would be free, (he himself) must strike the blow". What that means in very simple terms, and that's just his introduction, what it says to us in 2011, is that this world ain't gone give you nothing. And until you make up your mind to be a participant in your own progress, the one who has the WILLS to be free, you've got to be bold enough to strike the first blow...

Beloved, I need you to understand these words in context. In 1857, he was talking to a nation that was divided against itself north versus south and abolitionists versus the supporters of slavery. And while the two sides were fighting for the advancement of their own agenda, the message that he was really sending was to the colored folks who wanted freedom...

Look, here's the point as I see it. Frederick Douglas is telling us that if there a person who isn't willing to fight for himself, when he has a means of doing so, why anybody else should risk their life to jump in a fight that they're not even involved in...

Alright, let me put it REAL plain for you. While millions of people died for us to have the freedoms we enjoy today, what are we really doing to advance our own causes? Have all of us taken full advantage of those opportunities, or are we still blaming our oppressors for stuff we had control over?

Y'all have to excuse me while I talk to my people for a minute. Now, let me ask you these questions. Did white folks:

Make you run your credit up?

Make you spend more than what you had?

Make you buy eighty dollar shoes for a two year old?

Stop you from reading?

Stop you from furthering your education?

If not, why in the world, are we marching downtown against the government when the real enemy is right here in our own back yard!?"

Have you ever thought of the fact that when anything happens in anyone's life they are almost always present when it happens? Buddhist philosophy espouses that each action we take in the present has a direct karmic effect in the future. Buddhism states that humans have a conscious mind, a subconscious mind, and an unconscious mind. And they have different brain wave patterns ranging from conscious (when they are awake) to subconscious (light dream like state that communicates to us in our dreams) to unconscious mind (total deep sleep). As children, our subconscious mind houses beliefs and attitudes about life and about ourselves. These impressions, we pick up from society and people who have influenced us the most.

So, whatever the beliefs in our family and society at that time become our own. From these impressions we create thoughts and feelings about ourselves and our lives that are buried in the subconscious of our minds. So, if the biggest impacts in a people's lives were others that did not feel very good about themselves and felt life was supposed to be tough, then these too, become the people's own feelings and thoughts. From these thoughts and feelings which people subconsciously store they make conscious choices and decisions about what to expect and how they will live their lives. The problem, therefore, is that when we desire new experiences and positive changes, our subconscious can get in the way, there becomes a conflict, and the subconscious typically wins. Hence the statement "Be careful what you wish for, you may get what you want." It may not be what we consciously wanted; it just may be something familiar based on some feelings, events and beliefs from a long time ago (Duffy, 2010).

We all have the ability to choose our own destiny or path in life, but when it veers off in an uncomfortable direction, we are quick to assign responsibility to someone else. We do it in all sorts of ways. We blame people when mistakes are made at work, or take credit for others' work. We vent and take our stress out on others, and generally find fault before we look in the mirror. The problem with blame is that it is very disempowering and it rarely changes anything for the better. People cannot change their story when they are stuck in blame. When a person is stuck in the "blame mode," no effort on their part is required and, consequently, it elevates them to the status of being arrogantly ignorant, in as much as they hold the world responsible for their own happiness or poverty (Bren, 2010).

We would blame our family, friends, spouses, neighbors, pets, co-workers, boss, our kids, the government, the white man, the media, and the devil and so on and so on. We will blame just about everybody for why our lives aren't working the way they are supposed to. Our very nature in feeling entitled to have an amazing life, oftentimes leads to us not having one at all.

Entitlement is a conditioned feeling we have that everyone and everything is responsible for our success; a feeling of everybody owing us something good. And if we are not having any of it, it's because someone or something is responsible for our lack of happiness whether it may be in the home, work, relationships, or even the games we play. We fail to see that, may be, the real cause of our poverty or why our lives isn't working is the person who stares directly back at us in the bathroom mirror. We are solely responsible for the quality of the life we live (Baran, 2010).

Note that "Children are keen observers of parents. Even when engrossed in some activity, they will often pick up on mom's or dad's behavior, speech, and thought patterns" (2 King 21:19-22). Some of our behavior may be based on thoughts and feelings about ourselves and our lives that are buried deep in our subconscious mind.

Now, let's talk about some of the habits that blacks have most likely cultivated during slavery, which we continue to exhibit today and which may be contributing to our poor economic conditions.

The Role and Rituals of the Black Church

There are still many blacks who will raise their index finger, pointed in the air, when moving about in the church or any place of assembly. There is no doubt that many of us have observed this behavior in our churches and in any place of gathering with blacks present. I have actually seen some blacks do it in white churches. I wonder how many blacks really know the origin of this habit.

I have come to learn that this habit started during slavery. I was told by a ninety-two-year-old woman in Belle Glade, Florida that when slaves would go to Sunday worship service with their slave owners they had to obtain permission from the "Massa", the term used by slaves to refer to their owners, to go use the restroom. Upon approval, a slave would hold up their index finger as a way of announcing that they had been granted permission by their owner to leave. This behavior, I was told, was how law-abiding slaves were identified from those attempting to run away. Many blacks still make this gesture in gatherings today; unconscious of its meaning.

And what about the belief, still prevalent among blacks today, that black people are only supposed to wear their decent clothes on Sundays for church worship services? She told me that this is another belief leftover from slavery. During slavery, she said, slaves were only permitted to dress up on Sundays for church worship; the origin of the saying "wearing your Sunday best". Only black preachers were allowed to wear their "good clothes" on days other than Sundays.

Personally, I prefer to dress professionally, meaning a suit and tie, every workday of the week. I have been asked many times, by blacks and whites alike, why I am all dressed up on a weekday. Or, they will enquire if I am a preacher. Whenever white people, as well as a good number of blacks, see a well-dressed black person (especially a black male) during the week, the assumption is that he must be a preacher.

In my case, it almost never fails. Nowadays, when I am asked if I am a minister, my response is "yes." And the question that typically follows is "What church?" And my response is, "the Church of God here on earth." Then I will immediately follow with, "You know that each and every one of us was ordained for a ministry at creation and mine is in the classroom; I am a professor at the college." In most cases, they just walk away giving me that "you smart ass" glance.

Carter G. Woodson, in his book "The Mis-Education of the Negro," writes about the role of the black church in maintaining the slave mentality and behaviors among blacks today. He criticizes the church for focusing more on fire and brimstone rather than uplifting the people. He also considers the way blacks conduct church services to be an act of ignorance. He asserts that black preachers, today, have taken the black church and made it their own while continuing to maintain the servitude traditions that existed during slavery (Woodson, 1933).

Health and Wellness in the Black Community

Blacks are disproportionately represented in almost every disease that affects humans in this United States. There is the saying, "When America gets a cold, black America gets pneumonia." Our eating habits and lifestyle, which again can be traced back to the lifestyle during slavery, are greatly responsible for these diseases but most blacks have refused to acknowledge that their actions contribute to their poor health conditions.

During slavery, slave owners gave slaves the "throwaway" parts of slaughtered animal. For example, out of the slaughtered pig the slaves were given the skin, intestine, feet, ears, and head. If you noticed, these are the parts of the pig that contain the most amounts of trans-fats. With the skin, the slaves made pork cracklings; with the intestine they made chitterlings; with the feet and the ears they pickled pig feet and ears by putting them in vinegar; and with the head they made hog head cheese. I have also learned that the slaves used a lot of salt to preserve their meat. This probably explains why blacks like a lot of salt as seasoning in their food. Salt we know contains sodium which has been said to cause high blood pressure.

Blacks have been emancipated since 1863 and they are now in the twenty-first century—but we still eat like our slave ancestors did during slavery but fail to exercise and be mobile like they did. Our eating habits and lifestyle are killing us even though we don't have to eat like our enslaved ancestors did anymore.

The AIDS epidemic is a leading killer of black males. According to the United States Centers for Disease Control and Prevention (CDC), the prevalence of AIDS is six times higher in blacks and three times higher among Hispanics than among whites. In 1993, among children and adults, blacks were three to four times more likely than whites to be hospitalized with asthma, and were four to six times more likely to die from it. Available data indicates that the probability of dying from coronary heart disease (CHD) is greater in blacks than in whites and that there is a higher prevalence of smoking, hypertension, diabetes, prostate cancer, breast cancer, obesity, and left ventricular hypertrophy (LVH) among blacks. The truth of the matter is that blacks do not like going to the doctor until it is almost too late.

Tom Joyner's *The Tom Joyner Morning Show* has done its best, over the years, with its "Take a Loved

One to the Doctor Project" to enlighten and encourage blacks to go to the doctor for preventive medical check-ups. Many Blacks keep on eating those foods and doing those things that are killing them and have refused to modify their diet and lifestyle. An unhealthy people have a greater chance to be poor because they are not able to work full-time and afford the necessary medicine to keep them well. Blacks typically do not believe in preventive medicine. In my opinion, black people are the only group of people I know to hide their ailments from their physicians and expect to be healed.

According to government figures, nearly 50 percent of black women over age 20 are overweight or obese, compared with 33 percent of white women and 43 percent of Hispanic women. Dr. Regina M. Benjamin, the Surgeon General of the United States said during an interview at the 2011 Bronner Bros. International Hair Show in Atlanta said:

> "Oftentimes you get women saying, 'I can't exercise today because I don't want to sweat my hair back or get my hair wet. When you're starting to exercise, you look for reasons not to, and sometimes the hair is one of those reasons. The problem is that many women — particularly black women, like herself — invest considerable amounts of time and money in chemical relaxers and other treatments that transform naturally tight curls into silky, straight locks. Moisture and motion can

quickly undo those efforts, with the result
that many women end up avoiding physical activity altogether. I hate to use the
word 'excuse,' but that's one of them. We
want to encourage people, and also give
women the ability to look good and feel
good and to be empowered about their
own health..... Removing any barrier to
physical activity is crucial to the health of
American women, and in particular black
women, a group that has a higher rate
of obesity than any other demographic.
When researchers at Wake Forest Baptist
Medical Center in North Carolina sam-
pled 103 black women from the area, they
found that about a third exercised less
because they were concerned it would
jeopardize their hair. Of those women,
88 percent did not meet the Centers for
Disease Control and Prevention guide-
lines for physical activity, which is 150
minutes of moderate intensity exercise
each week, or about 20 minutes a day".
(O'Connor, 2011).

Violence in the black Community

Blacks seem to glamorize guns so much that toy
guns and B.B. guns are among the first toys they buy
their boys. These kids grow up playing with toy guns,
pointing and shooting at one another. I was in a rural

black church one Sunday in Gadsden County, Florida and there was a young boy, about four years old, playfully pointing a toy gun at other children around him, pulling the trigger and acting like he was shooting at them. This was during the worship service and this child was sitting between his mother and his grandmother. Neither of them seemed to notice what was going on and said nothing to correct this young boy's behavior. Why should they? After all, they allowed the child to take the toy gun out of the house and take it into the church. Yet we complain about drive-by shootings and the black-on-black homicide rate in our communities.

While blacks comprise 13.5% of the U.S. population, 43% of all murder victims in 2007 were blacks and most of the black murder victims — 93 percent — were killed by other black people. A study by the Bureau of Justice Statistics (BJS) found that from 2001 to 2005, more than nine out of ten black murder victims were killed by other blacks. In other words, of the estimated 8,000 African-Americans murdered in 2005, more than 7,400 were cut down by other African-Americans. Though blacks account for just one-eighth of the U.S. population, the BJS reports, they are six times more likely than whites to be victimized by homicide – and seven times more likely to commit homicide. In 2008, a total of forty homicides were committed in Little Rock, AR, 54% of which were committed by blacks against blacks. Nationally, homicide is the leading cause of death for black young men ages ten to twenty-four, and the second leading cause of death for black women ages fifteen to twenty-four.

I am going to just come out and say it. Black people kill other black people and people of other races over the dumbest stuff. There are numerous examples of these silly killings everywhere one looks in this country, both in urban and rural America. Remember the March 30, 2010 shooting in retaliation for Jordan Howe's murder in Washington D.C? Jordan Howe in attempt to steal a "gold colored bracelet," was murdered. On this fateful day in March, nine people were shot and four (ages sixteen to nineteen) of them were killed when a gunman opened fire Tuesday night, outside a southern Washington, D.C. apartment building. Police discovered that the victims of the drive-by shooting were returning from the funeral of their friend, Jordan Howe, when they were attacked. It is believed that Orlando Carter, who has been accused of the shooting, was shot after Howe's murder and that the Tuesday shooting was in retaliation.

In 1994, Rep. John Lewis (GA), who fought beside Martin Luther King Jr. during the Civil Rights Movement, very regretfully said, "Nothing in the long history of blacks in America, suggests the terrible destruction blacks are visiting upon each other today." Ninety years ago, Louis Sullivan, Secretary of Health and Human Services posed the question, "Do you realize that the leading killer of young black males in America is young black males? He went on to say that "As a black man and a father of three, this really shakes me to the core of my being."

Jesse Jackson, in 1993, said that "There is nothing more painful to me at this stage in my life than to walk down the street and hear footsteps . . . then turn around and see somebody white and feel relieved" (Jacoby, 2007).

What about the story of Germane Harris, who was killed in San Francisco some years ago after leaving his part-time job? The 33-year-old father of one was talking on the phone with his fiancée, Krystal Thomas, as he was headed to his car when the line suddenly went dead. Thomas said that "when his phone disconnected I didn't know what happened. He didn't try to call back and I was kind of waiting for him to get home. It wasn't until the next morning when he didn't come home that we figured out he had been shot in a drive-by shooting and, apparently, it was just something random."

On September 4, 2010 Chicago gang members held a press conference to blame law enforcement for the crimes and killings that are committed in the black community. These self-identified gang members also blamed poverty, drugs, and a lack of jobs for the problems in the streets of Chicago. They also said that Chicago Police Supt. Jody Weis' meeting with so-called gang leaders was a waste of time. (According to an exclusive report by the *Chicago Sun-Times*, Jody Weis, along with federal, state, and local law enforcement agencies, summoned local gang leaders, to a private meeting on August 17, 2010 under the pretense of a required parole session). But when asked what could be done right now to stop the daily barrage of bullets on Chicago streets,

Reginald Akeem Berry Sr., an admitted former gang member, said, "The problem with them is that they're giving us an ultimatum—quit—instead of an alternative. But we're offering these young men an alternative, saying, 'Get off the corner selling these bags, and come to this construction site and pick up this brick'." He and others at the press conference took issue with Weis's strategy of meeting with gang leaders and warning them of serious consequences if violence continues. Wallace Bradley, a Community activist and former gang member, told the *Chicago Sun-Times* that street violence is not always organized but often spontaneous. Another self-described gang member questioned how someone could be held responsible for the actions of another.

Blacks' Parenting Habits

There are many black parents who know for sure that their young sons and daughters are involved in drug dealing and gang activities but decide to look the other way. Let us be sincere with ourselves for just one moment. A parent has a young school-age child who has dropped out of school and is obviously not employed anywhere, but comes home and gives the parent plenty of money every so often. This child also frequently stocks the family's refrigerator with groceries, purchases a big flat screen television for the family room and maybe one for the parent's bedroom, and showers this parent with expensive gifts. And the parent doesn't ask where the child gets the money —what kind of a parent is this? But when this child gets arrested for selling drugs or killed in a turf war, this same parent wants to blame society for the loss of his or her child. No, do not put the blame on society; you should be blaming yourself as a parent for having failed your child in your parenting responsibilities.

About forty years ago, in a United States Department of Labor report, *The State of the American Work,* Daniel Moynihan sounded the alarm when he pointed out that "The collapse of black family life would mean rising chaos and crime in the black community. Today, up to 70% of black children are born out of wedlock and 60% are reared in fatherless households. And as reams of research confirm, children that grow up with unmarried parents and in dysfunctional and unstable families are more likely to engage in antisocial behavior". High rates of black violent crime are a national tragedy, but it is the law-abiding black majority that suffers from them most.

According to the latest report from the Violence Policy Center, the homicide rate for blacks in America stands at 20.86 persons per 100,000—nearly seven times the rate for whites, which stands at 3.11 per 100,000 persons. Indeed, 72% of black homicide victims were killed by someone they knew. And the weapon of choice is a gun. Specifically, 82% of the blacks killed in 2007 fell victim to a gun, usually a handgun. Based upon 1998 data, a fifteen-year-old black male faces a probability of being murdered before reaching his 45th birthday; that ranges from almost 8.5% in the District of Columbia to just fewer than 2.0% in Brooklyn, New

York. The probability of being murdered by age 45 is 2.21% nationally for all black males, compared to 0.29% for all white males.

History has taught us that no matter how poor black people were growing up, they always dreamed of becoming something and somebody. Even if they couldn't be it, they dreamed it anyhow. It is time to rekindle the dreams, the hopes, and the imagination of African Americans. I once heard Rev. Al Sharpton say that "This is the first generation of blacks that may give its children less than what it had". He pointed out that every generation before this found a way to give their children a better life than they had. "Our grandparents", he said, "had no money, couldn't vote, couldn't get well-paying jobs, and couldn't go on vacations but they reared their children to become doctors, lawyers, educators, judges, and even members of the U.S. Congress. During their time, they were "PO", poor without the "or", mainly due to circumstances outside their control, but today, we are "PO-OR" with the extra letters "OR" meaning that we now have a choice to remain poor. And too many blacks have chosen to play the blame game rather than taking charge of their lives. Black parents today have nice homes, nice cars, credit cards bursting out of their wallets, and numerous degrees hanging on their walls; yet they are rearing children who are walking around with their hats on backwards and their pants hanging down to the ground and falling off their butts, and unable to say three words without profanity."

Blacks in the Game of Politics

Majority of blacks have decided to disenfranchise themselves by purposefully deciding not to participate in this country's democratic political process. In playing the game of politics, blacks, for selfish reasons, may choose to dilute their voting power as a bloc by allowing too many blacks to run as candidates for the same office or barter their votes for political favors that are merely tokens. As a result, people who are really not interested in the black progressive agenda get elected to represent them. Troy Williams pointed out that African Americans continue to experience difficulties electing blacks, particularly in races outside of majority-minority districts. Unfortunately, and too often, the real political powers have continued to practice symbolic politics toward the black community by appointing a few blacks in high positions. Far from playing the brokerage role so skillfully performed by other politicians, many black politicians are viewed as agents of the machine by their peers. Hence, they choose to subordinate the interest of the black community to their own desires in order to achieve status, influence, and power as individuals through their association with white politicians or groups (Williams, 2010). Now that our actions have made it possible for the candidate who has no real interest in a black progressive agenda to be elected, we blame the government for ignoring black issues in the economic growth policy agenda.

If we really take a good look at the way blacks play the political game, we can conclude that the sentiment of some of those choosing to run for political office is, "I'm a black man without a conscience; if you need someone to dilute the black vote or become a double agent, I'm your MAN for a small fee." It is common practice, in the black community, to see people commit their votes to a political candidate in exchange for as little as a fish sandwich, a fifth of liquor, or small amount of money. Too many blacks are willing to give their votes away to a political candidate who comes to their neighborhoods and offers them chicken wing dinners and a limo ride to the polls. Many blacks don't care to take the time to learn the political platforms of candidates and aren't willing to listen to those who know and want to educate them. All they care about is that these candidates have promised to give them something—no matter how insulting the offer may be to the black race.

Furthermore, there are some blacks who actually allow themselves to be used as double agents, to the detriment of the black communities. For example, Lucy Morgan, senior correspondent of the *St. Petersburg Times* in Florida, reported that multiple lawsuits filed in Quincy, Florida claimed that white Gadsden County officials successfully conspired to remove or demote every black supervisor in county government. What's more, the suits say that an African American commissioner played a key role in the plot.

The report stated that the ringleader was another county commissioner, Douglas Croley, who was depicted as referring to black employees as "the Tribe" and was the only white on the five-member commission leading up to the 2008 election. In 2008, Croley conspired with Lamb, a black commissioner who has been on the board for seven years, to elect a second white to the commission. Croley and Lamb recruited two other men to run for the seat of black incumbent, Derrick Price. One of the recruits was Gene Morgan, who is white. The second was Randolph Bush, an African American. Bush's role in the alleged plot was to split the black vote. Bush only got 3 percent of the vote, but that was enough to enable Morgan to win by 64 votes.

Once they succeeded, the suits allege, the new commission majority of Croley, Lamb, and Morgan pressured a black county administrator, Marlon Brown, to resign. They replaced him with a white man, Johnny William, and gave him a "hit list" of black supervisors to fire in order to "whiten up" the staff.

It may be that too many blacks are hungry for attention and seem to be happy just to see that some attention is paid to them by candidates coming to their communities and talking to them. This sentiment is also obvious in the way that black preachers participate in the political process. Most politicians come to black churches only during election time; and when they visit, the pastor interrupts the singing of Amazing Grace to acknowledge them. In some cases, these politicians are invited to the pulpit to address the congregation. These practices of acknowledging visiting politicians do not exist in white churches at all. I have actually visited some black church, including the one of which I am a member of, where the pastors have delayed communion to give political candidates time to address the congregation or for themselves to sing praise of candidates, some of whom the pastors may know little to nothing about the history of their political activities in the community.

I am convinced that many blacks are not aware that the preamble of the United Sates Constitution of "We the people of the United States" did not include them when the Constitution was adopted in 1789. As a matter of fact, blacks were not included until very recently in U.S. History, only after many people sacrificed their lives and suffered tortures. The inclusion of blacks came from the civil rights struggles of 1940s to the 1960s. Frederick Douglas said that "If there is no struggle there is no progress . . . Power concedes nothing without a demand; it never did and it never will."

The apathy that blacks have toward democratic political participation can be argued to be one of the major reasons for the plight of black communities today. Too many blacks think that politics is a spectator sport. It is not; to win in the game of politics, blacks must actively play in it. President Andrew Jackson once said, "To the victor are the spoils of victory." A large number of blacks have the attitude of "as long as I am able to obtain the basic necessities of life I am fine and the affairs of the government don't concern me." Truly, I say that many blacks now suffer from the disease of amnesia that has made them forget how they got where they are today, or maybe, they are simply ungrateful for the lives that were lost and the sufferings that were endured to give them the privileges they now enjoy in this country.

Community Preservation

I am very sure that I'm not the only black person to notice how deplorable most properties and facilities in some black communities look. One behavior that is common in our neighborhood is how little we appreciate what we have and as such, treat the structures in our neighborhoods with utmost disrespect and disregard. It seems as if most blacks, adults and children alike, hate to see anything decent in our communities—a lot of us seem to cherish a life of deprivation and despair. We destroy or deface any unprotected and some protected structures in our communities for no apparent reason. For example, the government decides to build a recreation center, maybe with after school tutorial amenities in our communities, and in no time we begin to see the windows busted out with bricks thrown from the outside. The sinks and toilets in the bathrooms get busted with bricks or stone. Sometimes, old tennis shoes and other objects are stuck in the toilets to render them nonfunctional. Now that the toilets are overflowing and unusable, we begin to blame the government for the poor conditions of the center.

In many instances, the computers in these centers are either maliciously destroyed or stolen from the centers. This once beautiful building is defaced, inside and outside, with graffiti and all other kinds of inscriptions, some profane. Even when these centers are fenced to protect them from vandalism, the fence will be all torn down by community vandals. We seem to enjoy depriving ourselves, by destruction, of things we could use to enhance our progress or improve our quality of life so that we can continue to blame others for why we remain poor.

It almost never fails that after we have destroyed these facilities and amenities, we are quick to compare what we don't have with what is available in other predominantly nonblack communities. Instead of acknowledging the fact that we destroyed what had been provided to us to improve our quality of life, we start accusing the white man or the government of ignoring our needs and abandoning our neighborhoods.

Tardiness

Too many blacks seem not to understand the adage that "time and tide wait for no one." Blacks' subscription to a culture of procrastination (aka "I'm gonna") can very much be a factor in their poverty. Blacks have become so embedded in a culture of tardiness that they have created their own time zone: the Colored People Time (CPT) Zone. This is a mentally instituted time zone that blacks use to justify their lack of punctuality. Blacks have become so acculturated to being late that, if it were left to some individuals, they'd arrive late to their own funerals. This attitude of accepting tardiness as way of life can account for many blacks missing opportunities to improve their economic conditions.

Too many Blacks traditionally see nothing wrong with submitting applications late, turning in reports late, filing papers or documents late, showing up at appointments or events late, starting their own events late, and showing up for work late. When our tardiness causes us to miss opportunities or our applications rejected, we blame everyone else but ourselves for the failures. We must understand that procrastination is the greatest thief of time. When we procrastinate, we put ourselves in an unnecessary state of urgency and excitement that make us settle for mediocrity. Blacks must change their belief that the world will be at a standstill and wait for them to move before things begin. Rather than blaming the world for our problems we should, instead, always remember the saying, "If you snooze, you lose." The clock will keep on ticking and the river will keep on flowing.

I will dare to say that much of the "bad luck" that befalls us can be attributed to our culture of procrastination. Good luck is when the right preparedness meets opportunity. For example, to win the lottery, one has to be prepared by first picking the right numbers one believes are the winning numbers and playing them. And on the day of the drawing, if those numbers are drawn, then the person becomes the lucky winner. Failure to play the numbers is not being appropriately prepared for an opportunity to be a lucky winner. It is important for us to anticipate what is needed for success in any given situation and be prepared for when an opportunity arises. We typically wait until an

opportunity has come and gone before they start saying, "had I known, I would have, should have, and
could have." Blacks' tendency to wait until it is too
late to take action is responsible for their missing a
chance to succeed.

Here's a story about a friend of mine who was unemployed and claimed that he was seriously searching for
employment. In this story, I have changed the names
of the people involved to protect their true identity. I
am going to call this friend of mine Joshua Andrews.
Whenever I asked him if he had an updated resume,
his reply was, "I'll get one when I meet someone who
is hiring." I kept telling him about the importance of
being prepared because "opportunity strikes but once"
and he kept insisting on waiting to meet a potential
employer before he updated his resume. One day, as we
were riding in an elevator in the County Government
Building, we met a former classmate of mine at Florida
State University who also happened to be my fraternity
brother, Randy Phillips. Randy was the county administrator. After I introduced Joshua to Randy, I went on to
tell Randy about Joshua's background and that he was
currently unemployed and that he badly needed employment. Randy was surprised about the coincidence of
events since he was on the County Commission agenda
later that evening, in about three hours, to make recommendations for a position for which Joshua's background seemed very suitable. He asked Joshua to email
or fax him a copy of his resume to take a look at and
determine if it reflected what he was looking for to fill

this position. Randy promised to recommend Joshua for this position if his resume reflected the skills that the position called for. Joshua agreed to email his resume as soon as he got back home, but guess what? He didn't have an updated resume that reflected that his trainings and experience were truly fitting to this job.

When we got off the elevator Joshua started to lament how unlucky he was in life, how nothing ever went right with him. He even went as far as declaring himself "the most unlucky man on the earth." I hope you are not surprised to learn that he actually blamed Randy for not giving him enough time to prepare and send his resume. I am sure that many of you have, yourself, experienced, or know of someone who has experienced what Joshua went through.

The adverse impacts of the lack of preparedness in the black community remind me of the parable of the "Foolish Virgins" as written in the Holy Bible. The scripture states:

> "Then shall the kingdom of heaven be likened unto ten virgins, which took their lamps, and went forth to meet the bridegroom. And five of them were wise, and five were foolish. They that were foolish took their lamps, and took no oil with them. But the wise took oil in their vessels with their lamps. While the bridegroom tarried, they all slumbered and slept. And at midnight there was a cry made, behold, the bridegroom cometh;

go ye out to meet him. Then all those virgins arose, and trimmed their lamps. And the foolish said unto the wise, give us of your oil; for our lamps are gone out. But the wise answered, saying, not so; lest there be not enough for us and you; but go ye rather to them that sell, and buy for yourselves. And while they went to buy, the bridegroom came; and they that were ready went in with him to the marriage: and the door was shut. Afterward came also the other virgins, saying, Lord, Lord, open to us. But he answered and said; verily I say unto you, I know you not. Watch therefore, for ye know neither the day nor the hour wherein the Son of man cometh" (Matthew 25:1-13).

At this juncture, we know where the fault lies is of great importance, but what matters the most now is: what are we going to do to deal with all of the obstacles to our progress? We need to stop making excuses for why our lives are not going the way they are supposed to be going. We have to give up our need to be right all the time, our feelings of entitlement, the fear of failure, and the lack of motivation to eradicate our ignorance. We also must get rid of the mindset that we are victims of past circumstances—something someone said and/or did to us to cause us grief. We had no control over what happened during slavery but we now have the opportunities of which our enslaved ancestors never dreamed. Rev. Martin Luther King Jr.

once said that "Whenever men and women straighten their backs up, they are going somewhere, because a man can't ride your back unless it is bent"

Yes, we need to assume control of our lives and believe that only we have the power to dictate the direction our lives will be going and growing. It is important for us to believe that what we have from this point in our lives is what we can create for ourselves. We are now ultimately the architects of our fortunes and misfortunes. We should no longer be kept in fear when we remember and relive some past-based memories. We should no longer allow someone else's opinion or action to dictate how we feel about ourselves or our lives. We must stop allowing our circumstances to direct or dictate our lives. The winds of fate may blow us but we can still steer ourselves into the direction guided by our stars (Baran, 2010).

Jeff Jacoby writes that "The problem of poverty in black America is quite easy to solve. It isn't an insolvable problem. Black Americans overcame white racism; they can overcome black crime. But the first step, as always, is to face the fact" (Jacoby, 2007). Benjamin Elijah Mays, the son of a former slave, who came of age in the Jim Crow South, recognized at early age that if a person makes up his mind to succeed in life there is nothing that can deter him from achieving his goals. He believed that "He who starts behind in the great race of life must run faster to catch up with those ahead or forever remain behind".

CHAPTER FIVE

Jealousy and Envy

*"Happiness and freedom begin with a clear under-
standing of one principle: some things are within our
control and some things are not. It is only after you
have faced up to this fundamental rule and learned to
distinguish between what you can and cannot control
that inner tranquility and outer effectiveness become
possible . . . Remember, too, that if you think you have
free rein over things that are naturally beyond your
control, or if you attempt to adopt the affairs of others
as your own, your pursuits will be thwarted and you
will become a frustrated, anxious and fault-finding
person."*

—Epicetus

According to the urban dictionary, "crabs in a bucket"
is a syndrome where a group of like-situated people hurt those in their community who are attempting to get ahead. This is often applied to people in an

impoverished community where people start doing things that will get them out of poverty. The collective community becomes jealous or filled with a sense of self-loathing, so they find a way to pull those people back down to the community's level. When harvesting crab, the crab as a group will pull down any crab that starts to climb out of the barrel in an attempt to be the first out of the barrel that holds them, hence crabs in a bucket. This mentality is a way of thinking that is best described by the phrase "if I can't have it, neither should you." The example of this phenomenon in human behavior is that of a group that, out of jealousy and envy, will attempt to "pull down" (negate or diminish the importance of) any member who achieves success beyond the others.

The connotation of "crabs in a bucket" came from a fable that goes something like this: A bunch of crabs were sitting in a barrel at a seafood restaurant, waiting to be cooked. One of them said to the others, "Hey, you know what, if we all climb to the top and push on the lid, it'll come off and then we can escape." The other crabs all laughed. They knew it was impossible to escape. What could this foolish dreamer be thinking? It was nonsense. This couldn't be done. Not even worth trying. After a few minutes, when it was clear he wouldn't be getting any help, the one hopeful crab climbed up and started pushing on the lid alone. The other crabs just laughed harder, until they heard a faint creaking noise and realized that the lid was starting to shift a little. Then they all got angry. How dare one crab try to escape by himself? He was just another crab, and he needed to be shown that he was no better than the rest of them. So they grabbed the crab who had been trying to escape and dragged him back down to the bottom of the barrel. They all got cooked and eaten soon afterward, but at least they had the satisfaction of knowing that no other crab was able to achieve more than they had. While a single crab may find a way to escape, when several crabs are put in a bucket, none will escape. As one crab claws its way to the top, the others will pull it back down. This is a true phenomenon. Crab mentality is also a metaphor for the human response to self-improvement in others. Often when people see others advancing themselves, they subconsciously reach out to hold them back.

This term is broadly associated with shortsighted, unconstructive thinking rather than a unified, long-term, constructive mentality. It is also often used colloquially in reference to individuals or communities attempting to "escape" a so-called "underprivileged life," but kept from doing so by others attempting to ride upon their coattails or those who simply resent their success. This "crabs in a bucket" attitude of envy, hate, and jealousy that exists among blacks is reminiscent of the time of slavery, when the division among blacks gave birth to this mentality. During the time of slavery, often when one black person would achieve some freedom or success, other black people would do things that sabotaged the person's gains, thus pulling him back down before he made it out of his situation.

An anonymous writer told a story, in the February 11, 2008 issue of *AASPIRE magazine*, about a discussion amongst some people who were bashing various presidential candidates. Of course, it's not at all unusual around this time in a presidential election year; but one rant argued that Obama shouldn't be taken seriously because he was like "Superman . . . wearing his armor suit of ethnicity." Probably your first thought was that the author of that rant must have been a bigoted, cranky white guy. But the author of this article, who happened to be familiar with the guy, revealed that in fact he was not white, and he had a history as a very outspoken civil rights advocate; he was a black man. I was disappointed, but not surprised at that rant coming from a black since that sort of thinking has been so common in the African American community over the years. In this story, the civil rights advocate is a crab in a bucket that sees Obama as another crab in the bucket trying to achieve success.

Of course, I don't mean to suggest that this kind of self-destructive envy is in any way unique to the behavior in the African American community, because it is not. Just about every disadvantaged minority group expresses some version of it. Since this book is about black poverty, I am relating it solely to the black community because I see it in almost every aspect of blacks' attitudes and behaviors. This mentality, which is exhibited in the form of intra-racial discrimination within the black community, keeps black people in perpetual poverty. Some black people seem to think that if another black who happens to be a talented, well-educated professional accomplishes something worthwhile, it should not even be acknowledged because it might give the wrong impression. The commonly murmured comment in the black community will resemble, "Just who does this shiny 'negro' think he is, anyway? He must think he all that or better than all of us."

When blacks mock high black achievers for no other reason than their high accomplishments, it is an ugly and corrosive envy that is harmful to the community's progress as a whole. This likely explains why very intelligent youth in the black community will try to "dumb down" in order to gain acceptance or not be singled out by their peers. These kids see high achievement as "nerdish" or being "square"—something to disdain.

The people in our lives reflect who we are. In the different phases of life we may attract different types of people. As we grow and evolve as individuals the people in our lives will grow with us, fade away, or hold us back. We can influence others but we cannot change them. Change can only come from within. If we make the conscious choice to improve ourselves, we may also have to make choices about the people with whom we associate. This is not always easy. We do not want to leave behind the ones we love. Yet if they are not ready to make the same choice to evolve, we can either allow them to keep us from achieving our personal goals or we can separate ourselves enough from them in order to move forward. As we achieve our goals, we can offer encouragement and guidance. In any recovery or self-improvement program, it is recommended that you separate yourself from the people that you are used to being around because it is often those people that you were involved with in the behaviors you are working to overcome.

Any successful person will tell you they surround themselves with like-minded people. When we are surrounded by positive, motivated people, we lift up each other and propel each other forward. Wanting the best for others attracts people who want the best for us. Operating from a place of limitless possibility, we do not need to compete to be successful. We can rejoice in the success of others. There is a common saying that birds of the same feather flock together; sparrows don't fly with eagles.

The black community, however, does not promote the idea of limitless potential. It tends to act from a scarcity mentality. It seems as if the common frame of mind in the black community is to think that another person's success diminishes our own. We measure our level of success or failure in comparison to others. (Remember the "crabs in a bucket" theory.)

Mark Porteous tells a story about two longtime friends, John and Matt. They went to bars to drink and pick up women at least a few nights every week. They would laugh about being hung over and calling in sick for work. They did not have meaningful relationships with women. To both of them, women were merely a conquest. Eventually, Matt began to see the harm he was doing to himself—financially, physically, emotionally, and spiritually. He was sacrificing so many goals and desires for the same shallow experiences week after week. He decided he wanted to make a change. He told John that he did not want to behave like that anymore, that he was now determined to change his ways. Instead of encouraging Matt to better himself, John took it as an insult. He saw nothing wrong with the social rut they had dug for themselves. He was comfortable with the way things were—he did not want change. John tried to drag Matt down any way he could. He even used guilt to try to keep Matt from changing. Subconsciously, he was afraid that if Matt found happiness elsewhere, it would reflect a weakness in himself. Instead of seeing an opportunity for personal growth, he chose to hold his friend back (Porteou, 2010). Remember that misery always seeks company.

Bergen writes that:

> "People love success; they just don't like successful people. If someone doesn't care enough to help you find a solution, they should keep their mouths shut. I once worked with a safety consultant who was great at pointing out safety issues on site, but would never help with a solution. He wouldn't make a decision because he felt that he could be liable if he offered poor advice, even though that was his job. So he would point out problems, write a report about what shouldn't be done, and leave you to figure out what to do about it.

He thought that kind of performance was useless, and whether it was a
safety consultant or a nay saying family
member, if they aren't willing to be constructive and help you; you need to help
yourself. Don't rush blindly into something just because you want it, and I am
not discounting genuine concern. Pursue
your goals intelligently. Learn as much
as you can. Dive in and absorb all the
information possible, and then put it to
use. And never stop learning and apply-
ing, because that will constantly make
you better. You probably won't hit the
ball out of the park on your first try, but if
you keep striving, you just might be the
next entrepreneurial heavy-hitter in your
industry" (Bergen, 2010).

Todd A. Smith also narrated a story of how this
"crabs in a bucket" mentality negates progress in the
hip-hop community. He stated that:

"According to SOHH.com, a hip-hop
related website, "Young Buck performed
in Atlanta's Club Nocturnal. After his performance, Buck announced he had some
business to handle with Hot 107.9's DJ
Will, who was deejaying prior to Buck
coming on the stage. Although DJ Will
stood up for himself, he was outnumbered
by members of Buck's entourage who

jumped in. As a result, Hot 107.9 program director Jerry Smokin' B had to ban Young Buck from the station's play list." Young Buck's alleged assault led many deejays across the country to consider a ban of all of his music. Although rap music has always been highly competitive, many current rappers are unaware of the power that they have as role models, and choose to use their influence in destructive ways and not to uplift the black community. In past generations, African American youth emulated the preachers and the teachers. However, in the 21st century, the next generation of black leaders looks up to rappers and athletes for guidance and inspiration.

After the sudden deaths of Tupac and Biggie, many rappers realized the power of words. That generation of rappers understood the consequences of putting negativity on wax, and chose a more positive approach to settling differences. However, after the 50 Cent and Ja Rule (both of whom are rappers) beef (disagreements or quarrels) of 2003 became the talk of hip-hop, many rappers began seeing beef as a way to earn a quick dollar and destroy the career of an adversary in the process. Consequently, 50 Cent and his G Unit crewing began

beefing with Fat Joe, Jadakiss, and Nas
for their affiliation with Ja Rule and The
Inc. Records. After 50's protégé, The
Game, refused to participate in a battle
with Nas and Jadakiss, 50 Cents excom-
municated Game from G Unit Records.
Then 50 Cent went on a popular New
York radio show to announce The Game's
dismissal from the G Unit camp. After 50
Cent's diss (condemnation) on the radio,
Game's entourage attempted to confront
the G Unit entourage at the radio station.
The two crews exchanged gunfire, leaving a member of Game's crew injured.
After the New York radio incident, The
Game began exchanging countless insults
with the entire G Unit roster, culminat-
ing in the November 26 incident in which
Young Buck, a G Unit artist, allegedly
assaulted a deejay for playing Game's hit
single "It's Okay (One Blood)." Each rap-
per saw the others success as an obstacle
to their success hence they saw the need
to bring one another down".

Smith continued by asking:

"When will rappers ever learn? Hip-
hop culture has grown into a worldwide
multi-billion dollar phenomenon over the
years, and there is plenty of success to go
around for everyone. Just because a fan

buys a Game album does not mean this same fan will not buy an album from a G Unit artist. Young Buck's alleged assault in Atlanta has been a detriment to his career because of the ban of his records at many radio stations." In attempt to bring down an old nemesis, he may have brought down his own career in the process. According to Smith, "The beef that exists between rappers exemplifies the main reason the African American race has not been able to reach the potential that it has. A people filled with all the talent in the world cannot reach the "promised land" that Dr. Martin Luther King, Jr. spoke about because of their jealousy and envy" (Smith, 2010).

The Bible tells us in Galatians 5:21 that "Envyings, murders, drunkenness, reveling, and such like: of which I tell you before, as I have also told you in the past, that they which do such things shall not inherit the Kingdom of God."

In this country, too many African Americans have made poverty an acceptable way of life. We seem to be more comfortable with being consumers and depending on other groups for the goods and services we need. As a matter of fact, the black population is the only group in this country that is envious of its own hardworking or successful people. Blacks typically hate to see one another make it. Other races in this country make their members rich by developing their communities. For example, in Miami, the Cubans make Cubans rich; in New York, Jews make Jews rich; in Los Angeles, Asians (specifically Chinese) make their members rich. But in the black communities, we are so envious and jealous of our fellow blacks that we have nothing good to say about one another.

Too many Blacks are quick to criticize, bad-mouth, and have negative expectations of any one of us who is honestly struggling to live well. I overheard two young black men expressing their safety concerns, in one my flights from Tallahassee, Florida to Dallas, Texas—simply because the pilot in the cockpit was black. The passenger in front turned and asked the other one behind saying "Man, did you notice that the pilot is black?" The passenger behind responded with a sigh, saying, "Yeah, ooh boy! He's one of us. I hope he knows what he is doing." We do not have confidence or trust in the capabilities of other blacks compared to how we feel about whites doing the same thing. Blacks generally tend to subscribe to a "white is right" mentality. Black people need to realize that there are only twenty-four hours in a day. Our problem is that we spend so much of our time finding faults with other black people, being jealous of one another, and criticizing and bad-mouthing each other, that we do not allow enough time left to do anything productive for ourselves or about our state of poverty. Blacks tend to be so concerned about what others are doing and how they are doing it, that they ca not find time to worry about themselves and their own adverse situations. Let us remember that little minds talk about people and great minds talk about ideas. Blacks need to start talking more about ideas to improve their communities and less about other blacks who are striving to achieve greatness.

Another perturbing thing in the black community is that everybody in the black neighborhoods is in business but blacks themselves. Booker T. Washington asserted that "the only sure basis of progress is economics." He believed that the most effective means by which blacks could make a transition from slavery to full emancipation was through economic development. Hence, in 1881, he founded Tuskegee Normal and Industrial Institute. He urged former slaves to capitalize on skills they had used during slavery to establish businesses in their own communities.

How many people have gone to an Italian community and seen a Shiniqua Linguini store or gone to a Jewish community and seen a Malcolm X restaurant? In all the times I've visited Chinese communities around the U.S., especially in New York, I have not once come across a Marcus Garvey Kante clothing Store. Why is it that there are so many other ethnic groups owning and operating businesses in the black communities? Blacks have been frying chicken since they got to the United Sates, but have the nerve to still go to Colonel Sander's Kentucky Fried Chicken to buy fried chicken.

Victor Okafor, a professor of African American Studies, poses the question: "How is it that predominantly African American neighborhoods in Philadelphia are served by businesses owned and operated mainly by Asian Americans or white Americans?" This, of course, is what one sees wherever one goes into black communities all over this country. The Small Business Administration reported that in 2001, while there were 823,499 black-owned small business firms, there were 912,959 owned by Asian and Pacific Islanders, and 1,199,896 owned by Hispanics (Okafor, 1992).

In 1898, while on the faculty at Atlanta University, W.E.B Du Bois conducted a survey on African American-owned businesses. In this study, he revealed that African Americans had instituted an economic organization during slavery, based upon African traditions, which developed into businesses after emancipation. If this was the case, why is it that blacks can no longer organize and operate successful businesses in their own communities? My explanation is that blacks' dislike of seeing one another succeed keeps them from patronizing black-owned and black-operated businesses. Many people may be unaware that most of the black-owned businesses that succeed are not operated by blacks; the faces one sees in these businesses are non-black faces.

In this country, other races patronize businesses belonging to members of their own races. They circulate their money around in their own group five to ten times before it leaves. Have you noticed that in the black race, our money circulates within ourselves less than once? It's true. Only 6.6% of our money is spent with black-owned businesses. These same black businesses that we refuse to patronize are the very same businesses that we visit to solicit church or civic contributions. Blacks spend about 94% of their money with non-blacks. This means that 94% of our income is given away and only about 6% is kept. What must we do to build the economic base that we need to get our communities out of poverty? We must stop being "haters" of other blacks striving for success and self-improvement. Blacks must get rid of the "hook a brother/sister up" mentality whenever they patronize a black-owned business. When we patronize black-owned business, we should not expect to get anything without paying for it. After all, when we go to non-black-owned business we don't go there with an expectation of being given anything without paying for it.

Blacks starting their own businesses and patronizing them—not acting like crabs in a bucket—will enable us to take charge of our own lives and we will eventually shake off that hallow of political and economic enslavement that still hangs over our communities. We will provide employment for the people in our communities, our neighbors, and our children. This is how we can again begin to develop that sense of family that blacks once had. Above all, we will be able to change that "bad/evil" image that society seems to associate with people of the black race. Booker T. Washington once said, "One man cannot hold another man down in the ditch without remaining down in the ditch with him".

CHAPTER SIX

The Slave Mentality

"The moment the slave resolves that he will no longer be a slave, his fetters fall. He frees himself and shows the way to others. Freedom and slavery are mental."
—Mohandas K. Gandi

It appears that much of what is done and how it's done in the black communities is the same way it was done during slavery. The ideologies, philosophies, and mindsets that prevailed during slavery, to keep black slaves in check by the slave owners, are still prevalent in the way blacks do things amongst themselves today: to keep themselves in check. Blacks have not been able to totally free themselves from the slave mentality.

In his book, *Mis-Education of the Negro*, Carter Godwin Woodson writes that "If you can control a man's thinking, you don't have to worry about his actions. If you can determine what a man thinks, you do not have to worry about what he will do. If you can make a man believe that he is inferior, you don't have to compel him to seek an inferior status, he will do so without being told and if you can make a man believe that he is justly an outcast, you don't have to order him to the back door, he will go to the back door on his own and if there is no back door, the very nature of the man will demand that you build one" (Woodson, 1933).

Along the same line, Bob Marley's "Redemption Song" states: "Emancipate yourselves from mental slavery; none but ourselves can free our minds." Carter G. Woodson puts the same idea another way: "The race will free itself from exploiters just as soon as it decides to do so. No one else can accomplish this task for the race. It must plan and do for it itself."

Carter Woodson provides an overview of what he sees as the source of the invisible shackles keeping blacks enslaved in perpetual state of poverty. His idea of the mis-education rests on his conviction that the American education system has failed to present an authentic history of black America at all levels of education. He also argues that people are not willing to provide literature that deals with the black aspects and contributions in American history; and if they do, it is only superficial and in a "by-the-way" kind of way.

Any reference to blacks in American history is menial and dehumanizing, presenting them in subordinate roles. The references are utterly derogatory, primitive, or in devilish idol worshiping lifestyle of

African origin. There is hardly any available literature that presents black people's relevance in the building of America or Africans, in general, possessing any skills, talents, or abilities that have contributed to the building of America or world civilization. Woodson sees this neglect or distortion of the facts about black American history as a travesty of justice, deplorable and distasteful because it deprives the black community of its heritage by relegating them to state of irrelevance and nothingness. He asserts that any mis-education creates a vicious circle since the mis-educated person goes on to mis-educate others upon graduation. This generates a diminishing marginal education, which produces blacks that are ill-prepared to compete in a meritocratic society.

Woodson writes that "Negroes have no control over their education and have little voice in their other affairs. . . . Negroes are always such a minority that they do not figure in the final working out of the educational program. The education of the Negroes, then, the most important thing in the uplift of the Negroes, is almost entirely in the hands of those who have enslaved them and now segregate them" (Woodson, 1933). In my opinion, blacks have come a long way since emancipation; they now have the opportunity to have a voice in what their children learn and the fundamental values with which they are raised. But the question is, are the adults and parents in the black community willing to acknowledge the truth about black history? If blacks do not know their own history, they will not know what to say about their own affairs.

W. E. B. Du Bois puts it like this:

Negroes must know the history of the Negro race in America, and this they will seldom get in white institutions. Their children ought to study textbooks like Brawley's *Short History*, the first edition of Woodson's *Negro in Our History*, and Cromwell, Turner, and Dykes' *Readings from Negro Authors*. Negroes, who celebrate the birthdays of Washington and Lincoln, and relatively unimportant "founders" of various Negro colleges, ought not to forget the 5th of March—that first national holiday of this country, which commemorates the martyrdom of Crispus Attucks, an African-American Revolutionary War hero. They ought to celebrate Negro Health Week and Negro History Week. They ought to study intelligently and form their own point of view about the slave trade, slavery, emancipation, reconstruction, and present economic development.

Shackles in one's mind are far more challenging to lose than those that are visible from the outside. Cages clamped around a woman's heart are inconceivably more pernicious and difficult to escape than those in which she is physically locked. Chains wrapped around a man's soul are far more difficult to break out of than those wrapped around his ankles. Invisible bars nailed atop a black baby's crib are almost impossible for him to rise up from. You see, blacks were tricked by an evil force of slavery that taught them that they were less than human. Blacks were taught that they were less than everyone and everything. They were lied to and they believed it! There you have it and yes I said it. In the Bible (Proverb 23:7), we are told that "As a man thinketh, so shall he be." Our oppressors knew this from the very beginning of their campaign to use black labor to build their so-called New World.

The shackles of slavery were removed from the ankles and necks of black people in this country over 120 years ago, but because the shackles were not loosed from our minds, we continue to think and act as slaves. The shackles have now been moved to many other aspects of the black life. This is evidenced by the high percentage of blacks contained in prisons, the outrageous number of black males leaving black females to rear their children alone, the obscene rate of poverty and crime in the black communities, and the ridiculous numbers of black youth who refuse to be educated. Make no mistake; though there are blacks who have achieved some modicum of success, until we as a people are free, we are all enslaved (Scruggs and Lacey, 2007).

Shanique Jones believes that the mis-education of the negro that Carter Woodson writes about in 1933 was not an archetypical text of the past. Her position, like mine, is that it is just as relevant to the state of blacks in America now, as it was then. She asserts that though blacks have come a long way, the residues of slavery still linger in our communities and the educational spectrum. These residues, she believes, will continue to oppress black America unless blacks acknowledge the problem and work to amend it (Jones, 2007).

On July 9, 2007, the NAACP, in a mock funeral service in Detroit, Michigan, buried the N-word; it was supposed to rest in perfect peace. I was personally there to witness this truly emotional ceremony. The N-word has a historical bondage connotation to it. It was used and is still being used to disparage black people.

We get angry and feel insulted when people outside our race call us by the N-word because we consider it bigotry and dehumanizing; we get bent all out of shape. Since language is a representation of culture, in 2003, the NAACP convinced Merriam-Webster lexicographers to change the definition of the N-word in the dictionary to no longer refer to black people but instead to be defined as a racial slur. In the 1920s many blacks used the N-word, ending with an "a" (Nigga) as a pejorative term to denote class differences among themselves.

Many blacks today, especially in the hip-hop community, have become totally desensitized and as such have developed a culture they feel permits a casual use of the word which still excites rage and shame. They see the use of the N-word as a term of endearment. Even Rev. Jesse Jackson, who walked and worked beside Rev. Dr. Martin Luther King Jr. during the Civil Rights Movement, in 2008, disparagingly used the N-word in reference to Barack Obama.

Rev. Irene Monroe wrote that:

Language perpetuates assumptions about race, gender, and sexual orientation we consciously and unconsciously articulate in our everyday conversations and pass down through future generations. African Americans' appropriation of the n-word as insiders neither obliterates the historical baggage with which the word is fraught nor obliterates its concomitant social relations among blacks and between whites and blacks. Just because some African Americans use the term does not negate our long history of self-hatred. But what would work for us all is a history lesson, because reclaiming racist words like the n-word does not eradicate its historical baggage and its existing racial relations among us. Instead, it dislodges the word from its historical context and makes us insensitive and arrogant to the historical injustice done to a specific group of Americans. It also allows Americans to become unconscious and numb in the use and abuse of the power and currency this racial epithet still has; thwarting the daily struggle many of us Americans work hard at in trying to ameliorate race relations". She poses the question "Why is it that using an epithet, like the n-word — which was once hurled at African Americans in this country and banned from polite conversation — now broadly accepted in our society and culture today?" And I say, it is because many blacks cannot see the invisible shackles of slavery that make it so difficult for them to let their fetters fall (Monroe, 2010).

Looking at how most of those in leadership roles in the black community conduct themselves make me wonder: Are most of today's black leaders really leaders or are they just instigators? I see what many of the so-called black leaders are doing as being simply opportunistic; many of them emerge only when they see an opportunity to enrich themselves. To be honest, how many Dr. Martin Luther King, Jrs. do we really have left in our black communities? I once heard Rev. Al Sharpton say that "there are two kinds of leaders: the 'thermostat' leader and the 'thermometer' leader." The 'thermometer' leaders are those who feel the temperature of a room, take polls to see what is popular and benefiting to them before they take any position on an issue or do anything. They lack the guts to challenge the establishment for the good of a cause. On the other hand, the 'thermostat' leaders are those who will walk into a room and change the temperature by turning up the heat or turning it down. They are the leaders that will do whatever is necessary to change the norm for what is right. They are not interested in what they can get for themselves; their interest is the good of the cause. Today, we have far too many 'thermometer' leaders in the black community whose main interest is to pimp the black race for their own enrichment and they will not hesitate to do it every chance they get".

I have personally observed some of these self-proclaimed or white-ordained black leaders—all they do is come to the black community to tell blacks something but go back to those in power to say and do the contrary. These are the black people that are appointed to local advisory boards and committees, simply to add color to these groups. These very same blacks will make motions, second motions, and vote for motions that are outright detrimental to the black communities. Their motivation is "pimping" the black community for self-gains.

Sometimes, these blacks are sent by the blacks' oppressors to the black communities to convince them that some policies or actions, which everyone knows for sure are bad for the black communities, are actually good for them. For example, when a coal or biomass power plants, proven to have negative health, developmental, and environmental impacts, were proposed to be located in the black community, the people who were sent to sell other blacks on these projects were these "greedy" blacks. Though these blacks are active in our communities, their activities are almost always for their own gains; they do not really care about the general welfare of the black community.

There was another occasion when elderly blacks were about to be displaced from their homes in order to build holding ponds for water that flowed from predominantly non-black communities. It was obvious that many of the displaced elderly blacks couldn't afford to rebuild anywhere else. But would you be surprised to learn that these "black-pimping blacks" were the ones who were sent to these elderly citizens to convince them to sell their homes to the developers—knowing full well that that these seniors were about to be rendered homeless? Have you heard the saying, "All of your skin folk ain't your kin folk"?

Too many blacks are ostracizing themselves from mainstream America with their clustering tendencies. Segregation has been abolished in this country for a long time; so why is it that many blacks still feel that they can only associate with other blacks? There are some blacks who still truly believe that associating with people of other races constitutes selling out. The only time these blacks associate with people of another race is when they spend their money to purchase what they need from the non-blacks. When are blacks going to realize that the blind cannot lead the blind? If the blind leads the blind they are both bound to fall into the same ditch. Slavery kept blacks from integrating and as such kept them away from the knowledge that others were exposed to. Now that blacks are free to mingle with others, blacks should do just that, in order to learn some of what we need to know to make our lives and our communities better. Divisive language such as "them folks" or "people on the other side of the railroad tracks" keep blacks restricted to only what we know. Blacks need to step outside our comfort zones, expose ourselves to what exists outside our immediate communities, and stop being too comfortable in our ignorance.

At some point in American history, blacks were expected to go to the back of the room and sit at the back of the bus. But one day, Rosa Parks refused to move to the back of the bus. She went to prison and suffered to enable blacks to sit anywhere they wanted, including at the front of the bus. So why it is that today blacks still tend to gravitate toward the back of the room at assemblies? Just take a look next time you go to meetings or other places of gatherings and observe how many seats will be vacant in the front while blacks are crowded together in the rear of the room. The only place where you will observe blacks wanting to sit at the front is at a black church. When are blacks going to change this attitude of automatically relegating themselves to the back of the room to sit or to be served as they were expected to do during slavery?

Too many blacks exhibit what I call the "in-house slave" and "field slave" mentalities that still pervade the black community today. During slavery, those slaves that the slave owners take off the fields and bring into the house to perform housekeeping works tend to see themselves as better slaves than those still working in the fields. "In-house slave" here refers to blacks who have left the black community and struggled to attain some level of success, while "field slave" refers to blacks who are still stuck in black community with its deplorable conditions.

I am sure that many of us have experienced situations where blacks who are in some positions of authority (in-house slaves) talk to and treat other blacks (field slaves) like they are inferior to them and as such should be grateful to be in their presence. Many blacks are stuck on their titles and positions. Yes, too many blacks allow their titles, positions, or degrees dictate who they are and what they do. Just because they have some letters attached to their name, they think that it is now beneath them to go back to the communities in which they grew up. They now feel too good or important to speak to or interact with those they deem to be below their perceived status. They have become uppity with their nose turned up to those with whom they grew up around. Many blacks do not want to go back to their communities to share with those they left behind, who aren't yet as fortunate as they, how they got where they are. They think that just because they have earned some credentials, they are now insulated from the prejudices of America, and that staying away from the black community will ensure them that safety.

Deborah Mathis reminds us of how far from the truth that is. In her BlackAmericaWeb.com commentary she writes, "Ask the group of black Ivy Leaguers who were expelled from a downtown Boston club a week ago. By no account was there any misbehavior at their private party. Allegedly, the management of the Cure Lounge feared the high achievers would attract gang members, so they shut the party down on the pretext of 'technical difficulties'. Much was being made of the fact that the club goers were students or alumni of Harvard or Yale celebrating their university's annual football rivalry. Harvard, for heaven's sake! In truth, that was only relevant in the aftermath. Once a suspect is found to be a person of good repute—educated, productive, civilized, and law-abiding—it seems only reasonable to believe there was a bad call. But the problem is not credentials; it's color. What else made the Harvard and Yale celebrants suspects in the first place? And why is it more outrageous to make those assumptions about blacks who go to prestigious universities than it is to make them about blacks who go to community college or those who have taken pottery classes at the community center, for that matter? We don't wear our résumés on our faces. Quite obviously, it wouldn't matter if we did" (Mathis, 2010).

The flip side is that too many blacks judge others by the titles, positions, or degrees they possess. These are the people in the black communities who feel too inferior or unworthy to interact with blacks who have reached a socioeconomic level above the one that commonly exists in the black community. These less privileged blacks (field slaves) frown at any advice from those who left the community to accomplish a better life (in-house slaves). Poor blacks generally don't want to hear what well-to-do blacks have to say. They are so comfortable in their poor conditions that they will find reasons to condemn or reject suggestions from those who can relate to their current struggle and have succeeded in making their lives better. Yes, many blacks in poor black communities, especially the elderly, are quick at saying, "I am eighty-six years old and I have lived in this community all of my life. Who do you think you are to come and tell us that what we are doing is wrong? Just because you have gone somewhere and got some 'ga damn edumication' you now think you can come back here to tell us how to live our lives." And the young adult blacks in these poor black communities are quick at flaunting their generational legacy by making statements like, "I am a seventh-generation member of this community. I was born here and I have lived here all my life. Who do you think you are to come here and tell us how to do things differently? You were not even born here and if you were born here, you didn't even grow up here, so you don't know what you're talking about." They are quick to dismiss any ideas that may help improve the black community.

Assata Shakur asserts that "The black family during slavery was almost nonexistent. Siblings were often separated and on many plantations, many slaves competed for the favor of the slave master. Winning the favor of the slave master could mean securing a job as a house slave. It could also mean extra food, clothes, et. cetera. Thus, to many slaves, finding favor with the slave master meant that a slave had a better way of life. . . . the black family cut each other's (siblings) throats and refuse to support one another; spending their money with those outside their communities. Blacks often complain about these economic invaders of their communities." She goes on to pose the question, "Who is to blame for this intrusion? If black families and black people would cooperate with each other and support each other we would not have the influx of so many foreign businesses in our communities. Is the attitude of non-support of each other (even family members) a legacy of slavery, ignorance, or both?"(Shakur, 2007).

Personally, I think that if someone has lived in a community for so long or come from many generations of continuously destitute living conditions, that person should be more open to suggestions that will help improve their community. However, rather than welcoming ideas that will improve these poor black communities, these long-time residents will criticize and condemn any constructive suggestions so that they can continue to complain and blame everyone and everything else for their community's demise.

Another way that blacks contribute to their own poverty is through their inability to hold secrets. This behavior, I dare to say, is a habit cultivated during slavery. Many blacks still act like slaves during slavery by seeing themselves as being the one to leak any plans for freedom to the slave owners in hope of favors. Whenever blacks get together to discuss plans to improve their poor, black communities, there are always a few who will immediately reveal the plans in their infancy to those outside the community, especially those who would like to maintain the community's status quo of being exploited. If the plan has anything to do with freeing blacks from bondage of any kind, there are bound to be some blacks who, as soon as the meeting lets out, will tell somebody about what was just discussed at the meeting. We sabotage our own efforts for freedom; we just talk too much.

If our slave mentality continues to make us think from the position of weakness and stop thinking of ourselves as victims then we will be able to join forces to implement effective economic and social changes that will improve our communities. There is a saying that "If spider webs unite, they can tie a lion."

CHAPTER SEVEN

Ingratitude

"Ingratitude is a nail which, driven into the tree of courtesy, causes it to wither; it is a broken channel, by which the foundations of the affections are undermined; and a lump of soot, which, falling into the dish of friendship, destroys its scent and flavor."
—Giambattista Basile

To boast is to speak with pride, often excessive pride, about oneself or something related to oneself. I am a firm believer that having an attitude of boastfulness and ingratitude is an impediment to progress and happiness of any group of people. Also, people who are boastful of what they have, not seeing their possessions as blessings with which they can uplift others, inhibit progress in the community in which they live. These people, in the exhibition of ingratitude, demotivate others who now perceive the attainment of wealth as a curse that comes with misery.

On the other hand: gratitude, thankfulness, gratefulness, or appreciation is a positive emotion or attitude in acknowledgment of a benefit that one has received or will receive. People who show an attitude of genuine gratitude for what they currently have and what they are given do have greater opportunities to receive more and become happier and richer.

Scholars who subscribe to the Universal Law of Attraction claim that gratitude has the kind of vibration necessary to attract what one desires and to have more happiness and prosperity in one's life. This probably explains the saying that "Gratitude is wealth, wealth is gratitude".

An unknown author writes that:

"Gratitude' makes you focus on the things that are working in your life, which causes you to attract MORE of the 'good' stuff. Your ungratefulness makes you focus on the things you are ungrateful about, the things that are not working in your life—which means your entire focus is on what is NOT working in your life, the bad stuff, which causes you to attract more of the same undesirable result.

The Law of Life is the Law of Belief, also known as the universal Law of Attraction. It simply states that "what you deeply believe will sooner or later materialize as your physical reality". In other words, you are creating your own reality through the beliefs you deeply hold in your subconscious mind. And as you keep resenting and FOCUSING on the things that you BELIEVE are wrong in your life, the universal Law of Attraction guarantees that you shall keep attracting more of the same....Now, it should be perfectly clear why 'The ungrateful never prospers" (Law of Attraction Insight, 2011).

Mary Jo Kurtz wrote that "Giving thanks seems like such a simple idea, tossed freely about by habit. We teach our children to thank their friends for sharing toys, we thank co-workers for lending a hand on the job, and we squeal our thanks when opening birthday gifts. But when given sincerely and contemplated daily, those two little words have the power to change a household" (Kurtz, 2009).

As a child growing up in Nigeria, I was constantly reminded by my parents and elders that "the beggar's hand should always be more extended than the hand of the giver." This means that the recipient of a gift should put in more effort than the person doing the giving. I was taught as a child not to think that whatever I am given is owed to me by the person giving it. Rather, I must always remember that the giver is not obligated to give it to me. Gifts should be received with appreciation and gratitude since the giver is giving it to help me better myself. There was strong emphasis on showing an appreciation for a gift, no matter the size or what the gift may be. They continuously told us, "Always say 'Thank you' when you are given a compliment, as an appreciation for their kindness."

Another lesson that we were taught as children growing up was to "never complain of what we don't have or throw in the face of others what we do have." We were always reminded to be grateful for whatever we had. They put it like this: "A child complained of not having shoes to wear and thought life was unfair until the child went out and saw people without feet." So, we were told to "Never take what you have been given for granted; always show an appreciation and gratitude for what you have and do not brag."

As a matter of fact, I can recall several times when my parents would take back from us something they gave us simply because we did not say "Thank you." I remember one time when my mother took back a pair of shoes that she bought me for Christmas because she waited for me to express gratitude for the gift but I failed to do so. I did not get those shoes back and did not get anything else for Christmas. That was a lesson on the importance of gratitude that I have never forgotten.

I am sure that these same lessons were common parts of childrearing in the African American communities at one time in the past. Unfortunately, I have noticed changes that reflect a gradual erosion of these virtues of gratitude and appreciation among African Americans since I arrived in the United States in 1978. Older people tend to exhibit more of an attitude of sincere gratitude and appreciation than younger people in today's African American society.

Ingratitude

I will dare to say that the attitude of ingratitude and boastfulness, which pervades the African American communities of today, is one of the attitudes that contribute to the deplorable conditions in which blacks live. Grateful people have more positive ways of coping with the difficulties they experience in life, are more likely to seek support from others, reinterpret and grow from experience, and spend more time planning how to deal with the problem. Grateful people also have less negative coping strategies, being less likely to try to avoid the problem, deny there is a problem, blame themselves, or cope through substance abuse (Wood, et al., 2007).

Too many blacks are so suspicious of mainstream America that they think whenever they are given a gift; the giver must have some ulterior motives. This probably explains their attitude of ungratefulness, and their misuse and abuse of opportunities for progress. A.M Wood, et al., stated that "Gratitude is an emotion that occurs after people receive help, depending on how they interpret the situation. Specifically, gratitude is expressed if people perceive the help they receive as (a) valuable to them, (b) costly to their benefactor, and (c) given by the benefactor with benevolent intentions (rather than ulterior motives)"(Wood, et al, 2007).

Studies have shown that there exists a correlation between gratitude and well-being. Grateful people are happier, less depressed, less stressed, and more satisfied with their lives and social relationships (McCullough, et al., 2002; Wood, et al., 2008; Kashdan, et al., 2006). Grateful people also have higher levels of control of their environments, personal growth, purpose in life, and self-acceptance (Wood, et al., 2009).

The findings in an experiment conducted by R.A. Emmons and M.E. McCullough (Emmons & McCullough, 2003) support the correlation between gratitude and well-being. This experiment was carried out with three experimental groups over a period of ten weeks. Prior to the experiment, the participants were instructed to keep daily journals that recorded their moods, physical health, and general attitudes toward life. These journal entries were used to provide a pre-test and post-test for the experimental intervention.

1. The first group was asked to write down five things they were grateful for that had happened in the last week for each of the ten weeks of the study. This was called the gratitude condition.
2. The second group was asked to write down five daily hassles from the previous week. This was the hassles condition.
3. The third group simply listed five events that had occurred in the last week, but not told to focus on positive or negative aspects. This was the events or control condition.

The types of things people listed in the grateful condition included:

- Sunset through the clouds
- The chance to be alive

- The generosity of friends

And in the hassles condition:

- Taxes
- Hard to find parking
- Burned my macaroni and cheese

People who were in the gratitude condition felt fully 25 percent happier—they were more optimistic about the future, they felt better about their lives, and they even did almost 1.5 hours more exercise a week than those in the hassles or events condition. The same study revealed that people who exhibit gratitude are more likely to make progress toward personal goals, including academic and health-based goals, when compared to others.

Kate Judd declares that "gratitude is an open door." In this declaration she told three stories about wealth and poverty. In one of the stories, she talks about two of her friends who had never met each other:

> They were close in age. They were each divorced; they came from the same ethnic background. One had one teenager, the other had three. They shared many interests. I thought they would love each other.
>
> At a party at my home, I introduced my friends to each other. "Annette, this is Barbara; Barbara, Annette. You have so much in common."

Annette was a talkative type. Right
away, she began to tell Barbara about her
life. "It's so tough being divorced, isn't
it?" Annette said. "I mean, money is so
tight. My new house cost two hundred
and seventy thousand dollars. I had to get
financial help from my father. It's not that
Daddy doesn't have it—he just endowed
a chair at a major university. But I hate to
ask. Of course, I do have the alimony from
Bill, my ex; but I don't feel that I should
rely on that. I'm putting it away for my
retirement—that's what my accountant
says I should do. And the house that Bill
and I built just won't sell. I don't know
why. We spent nine hundred thousand dollars on that house, it's absolutely perfect.

"It doesn't matter so much to Bill if
the house doesn't sell. He's the vice president of a big bank in the city. But I'm
really struggling. I mean, I don't make
much. I'm just a music teacher. So, anyway, what I've decided to do is build
an addition onto my new house: a little
apartment. I don't know where I'm going
to come up with the money. It's going to
cost sixty thousand. But, you know, it's a
tremendous investment in the long run. It
adds to the value of the house. And I'm
going to rent it out, so then I'll have the

rent every month to add to my income. It's worth it to scrape a little while I'm having it built."

My friend Barbara sat silent. She had a smile fixed firmly on her face. I had never heard Barbara say anything unkind about anyone—ever. She never said a word against Annette, either; but after the party, she told me she would prefer not to see Annette again.

You see, I had forgotten one thing: while Annette, who was worth several hundred thousand dollars, worried about whether she had enough to survive, Barbara was supporting herself and her teenage child on ten thousand dollars a year, which she earned by mopping floors and scrubbing toilets. And she never complained.

Judd points out that "Before this, what had she thought about wealth? About poverty? I had grown up in comfort, never lacking for any material thing—indeed; indulged in anything money could buy. I had known that there was a difference between me and most of the other children at the tiny rural school where I had gone as a child. But I had not realized that the difference had to do with money. Like many a young member of the upper classes, I did not know what I was."

She continues to say, "Sitting with Annette and Barbara, I knew. I thought, '"Let me never take what

I have for granted. Let me never complain about being poor, when I am really rich.'" Judd, continuing with the story, writes:

> If you had asked Barbara if she was poor, she would probably have denied it. She would have said, "I have a child who loves me. We have a house to live in. I have my health, so that I can work for my living. Sure, we have to get food from the Community Pantry sometimes, but we always have enough to eat. I'm even able to scrape together enough to go to school, so that someday I'll be qualified for a better job which still allows me to take care of my emotionally troubled child. I have a family who cares about me. I'm thankful to have so much." Judd concluded this story by saying, "Maybe I should take Barbara for an example? Maybe I should be grateful for what I have—however much or little it is."

Judd's second story goes like this:

> I have a middle aged relative who lives alone in a large house. Mentally somewhat disabled, she does not work, but is supported by a large trust fund set up by her late parents. Though her life style is not opulent by North American standards, she is always beautifully dressed, well

fed, and can afford to hire people to do any job she cannot, or does not wish to do herself.

One day my relative went to the super-market (how much we take for granted)! Another friend of mine once hosted a professor from Russia. The professor was overwhelmed and enchanted by the small local supermarket. She exclaimed, "In America, your markets are like muse-ums!" My relative, her eyes glazed and her feet sore after a long trip through the abundantly stocked aisles, decided to go to the flower case and pick out a refresh-ing bouquet for herself. In front of the buckets overflowing with big, richly colored roses stood an old Asian woman, who was silent as my relative selected her flowers. "So cheap," my relative thought. "Only a dollar a stem!" She chose a large bunch.

The other woman still stood there. "It's hard to pick, isn't it?" my relative said. "Oh, I cannot buy any," said the old woman. "Too expensive. I only like to come and look. They are so beautiful."

So this woman was grateful for the free beauty of flowers in a supermarket/museum. Was that all? Did she feel her poverty, in not being able to afford a one dollar rose? There are those who would argue that this woman was wealthier than my friend Annette, who has a great deal of money but feels always impoverished. In this case, my relative should not have felt any guilt or worry, but should have taken her flowers home and enjoyed them, secure in the notion that we must each simply be thankful for what we have, no matter how we came to have it. Or should my relative have offered to buy some flowers for the old woman? That is another popular solution: those who have more should make private donations to those who have less. Perhaps my relative should have put her own flowers back in the case and donated her money to some worthy organization—one which fights poverty?

Judd, in her third story writes,

Once, I saved up my money all year long so that I could go to a workshop. The workshop took place at an institution that specialized in "self-actualization," "spiritual exploration," "natural healing," and so forth. At this institution there were perhaps a few hundred people who had come to take workshops in pursuit of these vague but laudable goals. Among them I saw perhaps ten who were not white.

Although it was more difficult to tell, I would guess that there were equally few who were not economically quite well-off. Although I come from "the whitest state in the union," I felt uncomfortable with this lack of ethnic and class diversity. Still, I quite enjoyed the workshop I was attending.

One night I was standing in the dinner line next to the person who was presenting the workshop, a woman of extraordinary power and charisma. She stretched her arms akimbo and proclaimed in a loud voice, "Ah! It's good to be alive!"

Judd continues:

Something must have registered on my face. Perhaps I drew slightly away from her. I know that for the rest of the workshop, she looked faintly displeased with me. But you see, I was thinking, for *you* it is good to be alive. For *me* it is good to be alive. But what about the homeless person who is sleeping tonight in a public park? What about the person who has just discovered they have cancer, and have no health insurance to cover treatment? What about the residents of other, less wealthy countries—the man who lives in a tin shed in Mexico, the woman who begs in the streets of Bombay? What about the

children who are starving, and the moth-
ers who cannot feed them? Just what do
you mean, "it's good to be alive?!"

Judd's conclusion was that gratitude is an open door
to the next step. She said, "I can open that door of gratitude, and walk forward, doing what I can to help others achieve what I have. Or I can close the door. Then
gratitude becomes complacency, and I am trapped."
(Judd, 2000). Each of these stories gives us reasons to
be always grateful and teaches us to be appreciative
of what we have; we must not think that it is always
greener on the other side.

The exercise of ingratitude is mostly noticeable in
the African American communities during the holiday
seasons. This is the time when civic organizations prepare gift baskets that they deliver or distribute to the
less fortunate families. These gestures are acts of char-
ity but all too often those receiving these packages have
attitudes of entitlement.

In my community, like every community in the
United States, it is very common to see gift baskets
being delivered to the less fortunate families by various
benevolent organizations.

The purpose of this, I would imagine, is to give
these families an opportunity to share in the festivi-
ties of that season. I have been a part of some of the
organizations that do this charitable giving during the
holidays. The lack of gratitude that I observed among
African Americans in my community was outright
despicable.

There was one time when a local university in my community decided to give a helping hand to parents before the start of the school year, by giving them a $15.00 gift card per household toward school supplies. I was amazed by the attitude of a lot of the parents at the distribution site. Over and over again, we heard parents complaining that the amount on the gift card was not enough to cover the cost of their children's school needs. I heard a parent say, "How do they think that this little money can cover what I need for my children? I have five children and I am a single parent. The government don't do a damn thing as it is. Even ten of these cards will do me no good." They wanted the university to do more by giving them multiples of these $15.00 gift cards or increasing the amounts on each card. Some parents actually made attempts to obtain multiple cards by sending their children back to the distribution table with instructions to say that their parents were not able to come and they were there to pick up their gift cards.

I hope you are not surprised if I tell you that some parents actually tossed the gift cards back at the person passing them out and walked away in anger, spewing profanity as they left. I was more interested at the number of parents who said "Thank you" upon receiving a card. I was utterly surprised to see the number of times when parent received a gift card and just simply walked away without saying "Thank you." The expression of gratitude came more from older parents than younger one. Most of the young parents walked away in indignation. I would like to mention that the university has continued to do this act of charitable giving to help the families in the predominantly African American schools in the community. This is the area of town that this university is located.

At another occasion involving the distribution of Christmas baskets by another one of my clubs that annually gives out a Christmas package consisting of a frozen, whole turkey (20-30 pounds), a bunch of collard greens, a five-pound bag of potatoes, and a paper grocery bag full of items needed for a feast.

Each year, the club members contact the local churches and organizations to find people that may need help with food to celebrate the Christmas holiday. The churches in turn make a series of announcements asking members who may need a Christmas basket to please contact the church office to register.

This announcement is also advertised in the local newspaper and broadcasted on some of the local radio stations for several weeks. The announcements provide contact information to register for these baskets. This process is started in late July to early August of every year. Upon contacting the churches and organizations, a return stamped postcard is given or sent to the applicant. All the applicant needs to do is complete this postcard, providing their name, address, contact telephone number, and whether they would like their package delivered or they would like to come and pick it up themselves on the day of distribution that is specified on the card. Eligibility is not ethnicity-based; this project provides assistance to all citizens in the community.

But what never ceases to amaze me, in the few times I have been a part of this event, is that on the day of the distribution in the month of December, I am sorry to say that the people we have typically had problems with just happen to be blacks. Other blacks, who are members of this organization, by the way quite few, have gotten me to understand that the situation with blacks' attitudes on the days of distribution has been the case for a long time.

The few white applicants (most of whom opted for their packages to be delivered to their homes), the many Latinos, and nearly every older black person who came through the line received their package with a "Thank you" and some more words of gratitude. However, most of the younger blacks (males and females but especially the males) just got their packages and left; no thank you or any expression of appreciation. Some even asked for two turkeys and extra bunches of collard green just because they saw a truckload of turkeys and a trailer full of collard green. I remember this one woman with three children, who asked for two packages because one would not be enough to feed her family of eight children and her mother. Her argument was that her mother deserved her own package.

Now, are you ready for this? When the club members in charge of this project refused to give her another package, she told them they should be ashamed of themselves for trying to keep what the government has given the club to distribute to the poor for themselves.

She stormed away in anger, yelling loud and excessive profanity.

There are occasions when some people who returned their postcard with the instruction for their packages to be delivered to their homes, came by the distribution site to collect another package. Some of them adamantly argued that they had not requested that their packages be delivered to their homes and as such must be given their package. In each of these situations, the organizers went into the pile of returned postcards to show that they indeed requested that their package be delivered and it has been delivered or will be delivered. There was one particular case where the young man became very loud and belligerent. It was so bad that we had to contact the club member who delivered the package to his home to confirm that the package had already been delivered. Upon putting the young man on the phone to speak with the member, we discovered that this young man actually was the same person who took delivery of the package at that address.

And there were a number of situations where the people came for pick-up but their cards were never returned as instructed. Mind you, the deadline for returning the postcard was boldly printed on the card. The issue is not that they mailed their postcard and the club hadn't receive it. They brought their postcards with them on the day of distribution. This means that they were not in the head count for the packages that were prepared. I am not sure if you really want to hear how some of these situations went; they were ugly.

Some members of the club actually suggested that the club terminate this Christmas Holiday Gift Basket Project. Their justification was that it was becoming dangerous and "those people" were beginning to think that we owed it them.

It is very important that I mention that there were some blacks who were very emotional in their expression of gratitude. Some, especially the elderly, prayed and called on God to forever bless the club and its members for the good it does. There were some that could not stop giving hugs and kisses for what they received.

Having an attitude of gratitude is very necessary for people to be able to attract and manifest those good things that they desire to happen in their lives. The development of an attitude of gratitude to foster growth and progress in a person's life is prevalent in all theological teachings. Gratitude is viewed as a prized human prosperity in the Christian, Buddhist, Muslim, Jewish, and Hindu traditions (Emmon & Crumpler, 2000).

Many believe that the entire life of the Christian is molded and revolves around gratitude. Martin Luther referred to gratitude as "the basic Christian attitude" and it is referred to today as "the heart of the gospel" (Emmon & Kneezel, 2005). Gratitude in Christianity is an acknowledgement of God's generosity that inspires Christians to shape their own thoughts and actions around ideals. Instead of simply being a sentimental feeling, Christian gratitude is regarded as a virtue that shapes not only emotions and thoughts but actions and deeds as well (Edmmon & Crumpler, 2000). Mary

Baker Eddy, who established the *Christian Science Monitor*, put it this way: "Are we really grateful for the good already received? Then we shall avail ourselves of the blessings we have, and thus be fitted to receive more" (Eddy, 2011).

Gratitude is also seen as a vital part of the lives of the followers of Judaism. The Shema, a Jewish prayer, is an expression of gratitude. Alenu, the Jewish concluding prayer, talks of gratitude by thanking God for the particular destiny of the Jewish people. Along with these prayers, faithful worshipers recite more than one hundred blessings called Berakhots throughout the day (Edmmon & Crumpler, 2000).

The idea of gratitude is all over the Quran. Islamism encourages its believers to show gratefulness and give thanks to Allah in all circumstances. The teachings of Islam emphasize the notion that people who are grateful will be rewarded with greater pleasures. The Pillar of Islam that calls for daily prayer encourages believers to pray to God five times a day in order to thank him for his goodness. The pillar of fasting during the month of Ramadan is for the purpose of putting the believer is a state of gratitude (Edmmon & Crumpler, 2000).

In my opinion, Wes Fessler's take on this issue of gratitude sums it all up. He writes, "A thankful heart is never half full or half empty, but always overflowing with love. In difficult times when we are confronted with adversity, we can be blinded by narrowing visions of darkness that cloud our view with negativity. To be thankful for all of our experiences, we must be willing to work toward gaining something positive from every day. Thankfulness is a process, not an overnight trans- formation" (Fessler, 2010).

People create their own realities through the beliefs they hold in their subconscious minds. And if blacks can cultivate an attitude of genuine gratitude for what we currently have and what we are given, I believe that we will begin to have access to greater opportunities to receive more happiness and wealth that will enable us to focus on bringing about economic and social prosperity to our neighborhoods.

Epilogue

"In order to succeed, your desire for success should be greater than your fear of failure."

— Bill Cosby

I truly believe that the state that many people find themselves in is a matter of choice. Acknowledging our faults to improve our state of affairs means that we are taking responsibility for the bad choices we have made to create the bad situations in which we find ourselves. This acceptance of responsibility for our actions can be one of the most difficult things in our lives to grasp. No matter how small or big the situation might be, to look within oneself for the things that we have done to contribute to the situation we are in can really become one of the hardest pills to swallow. Most people feel good about themselves if they can blame something or someone else for their own problems. To be accountable for our problems is like pointing the finger at ourselves for our own failures; it is an acknowledgement of our own imperfections and weaknesses. Too many people are too self-indulgent and righteous to go this route. All I am saying is that we have to face our problems before we can fix them.

Most people feel that acknowledging their faults reduces them to a level beneath what they desire to be. So, they take the easy way out. This probably explains why many of us become adamant in our denial of faults and refuse to accept responsibility for our actions that may be obstructing our progress. We must be aware that blaming others does not give us control of our own lives.

By acknowledging our faults and getting to their roots, we can come to terms with our responsibilities and begin to do what we must do to improve our lives and our communities. Unless we want our future to be fettered by our past faults it is imperative that we own up to our shortcomings. The Law of Attraction promises that people can change their lives and conditions under which they live whenever they choose to make those necessary changes. If we are not willing to acknowledge our faults, it means we are not willing to accept the fact that we have made mistakes in our lives. If we cannot do that then we will be stuck in our present state of poverty or misery.

It is imperative that we as black people become serious about addressing the state of affairs in modern black America. Acknowledging our faults is the first barrier that we must overcome before we can begin to deal with the poor social and economic affairs of the black community. In this book, I have attempted to do just this, by focusing on how our own thoughts and behaviors may be helping to create our present state of existence in a nation blessed with so much abundance. Each of the seven chapters is an attempt to draw attention to an area in which the beliefs and actions of blacks contribute to the state of affairs in modern black America.

Too many blacks have become comfortable with the patterns of behavior that have created the present deplorable state of affairs in the black communities. As a matter of fact, these detrimental patterns of behavior have become so entrenched that they are now part of the African American culture. This could explain why it might not be easy to implement the changes needed to change our state of affairs. Very few of us look forward to making major adjustments in our life patterns. Once we become comfortable with how our lives are working, even if they aren't; it can be very upsetting to have them changed by someone else, or make the changes ourselves. No one likes to be out of one's comfort zones. How can we make changes that aren't uncomfortable? (Miller, 2009)

The more African Americans are able to gain control of their subconscious minds and begin to acknowledge the power of positive thinking, the more I am convinced that they will begin to change the state of affairs in the black communities for the better.

We need to look at what we have been doing that has not worked and then quit doing it. We must be passionate about what we do, who we hang with, or what

we are accomplishing in life. If our diet has perpetu-
ated a hereditary propensity toward Type 2 Diabetes,
continuing to eat the same foods will not cure the problem (Miller, 2009). Since most of the things people do
in life are influenced by what they observed from their
surroundings, blacks must now change how they live in
their communities.

If I may borrow the words of Frederick Douglas in
his July 5, 1852 *What to the Slave is the Fourth of July*
speech, I would say "Dealing with the issue of poverty
in the African American community needs "fire" not
light on the subject; "thunder" not a gentle "shower" of
reason". We should indict the black community on the
issue of its poverty like Douglas indicted our nation for
celebrating freedom and independence, while keeping
slaves. Douglas also once said that "Those who profess
to favor freedom and yet depreciate agitation are people who want crops without ploughing the ground; they
want rain without thunder and lightning; they want the
ocean without the roar of its many waters."

I hope and pray that each of the seven chapters in
this book has awakened the consciousness of black
America to some of what it does to contribute to the
demise of its people. Rather than vilifying my daring
to write about this part of the black life, let us use this
book as a catalyst to start a dialogue on how to improve
the lives of black Americans. It is time for the black
community to take responsibility for its actions and
focus on how to make the changes necessary to bring
about an improved quality of life. An awareness of how

Epilogue

we as black Americans contribute to our own poverty and state of affairs may lead to behavioral changes that will break the cycle of multi-generational poverty in the black communities of America.

Bibliography

Amaga, Sam. *Committed to the End.* Lagos: Aslove Publishing House, 2007.

Andrews, Marcellus. *The Political Economy of Hope and Fear: Capitalism and the Black Condition in America.* New York: New York University Press, 2001.

Aston, N.M, and S.S. McLanahan. "Family Structure, Parental Practices, and High School Completion" *American Sociological Review*, 1991.

Baran, Suzanne. "Own Up to Yourself: Stop Playing the Blame Game" *California Psychics,* 2010.

Bergen, Jake. "Crabs in a Bucket" *Ezine Articles*, 2010.

Bell, Derrick., *Faces at the Bottom of the Well: The permanence of Racism.* New York: The Perseus Books Group, 1992.

Borja, Raymond. "Stop Playing the Blame Game and Take Control" *SelfGrowth.Com*, 2010.

Bren, Kathleen. "Change Your Life Story: Stop Playing the Blame Game" *SelfGrowth.com*, 2010.

Bridges, Annette. "Stop Playing the Blame Game," *The Huntsville Item*, June 25, 2010.

Charles, Kerwin Kofi et al. "Conspicuous Consumption and Race," *An Abstract*, 2007.

Clark, Kenneth B. and Mamie P. Clark, *Racial Identification and Preference in Negro Children*, 1939.

Cosby, William H. "Public Criticism of Parenting Practices," *Gala at Constitution Hall, Washington, DC*, 2004.

Davis, Kiri. "A Girl Like Me" *Documentary*, 2005.

Dollard, John., *Cast and Class in a Southern Town*. New York: Doubleday Anchor Book, 1937.

Dombeck, Mark and Wells-Moran, Jolyn. "Methods for Changing Your Relationships," *MentalHelp.net*, 2006.

Dombeck, Mark and Jolyn Wells-Moran. "Changing Your Knowledge, Skills and Abilities and Credentials," *MentalHelp.net*, 2006.

Douglas, Frederick. "What to Slave is the Fourth of July?" *Speech in Rochester*, July 5, 1852.

D'Souza, Denish., *The End of Racism: Principle for a Multiracial Society*, New York: Free Press, 1995.

DuBois, W. E. B. "Does the Negro Need Separate Schools?" *Journal of Negro Education* Volume IV No. 3, July, 1935.

Duffy, Erika. "Taking Control of Your Life" *About. Com: Holistic Healing*, 2010.

Eddy, Mary Baker. "What's There to be Grateful for When I'm Sick", *Science and Health with Key to Scripture*, Mar. 30, 2011.

Emmons, Robert Ą. and Cheryl A. Crumpler. "Gratitude as a Human Strength: Appraising the Evidence." *Journal of Social and Clinical Psychology* 19.1 (2000): 56-69.

Emmons, R. A., & McCullough, M. E. "Counting Blessings versus Burdens: An Experimental Investigation of Gratitude and Subjective Well-being in Daily Life." *Journal of Personality and Social Psychology*, 84(2) (2003) 377-389.

Emmons, Robert A., & Cheryl A. Crumpler. "Gratitude as a Human Strength: Appraising the Evidence." *Journal of Social and Clinical Psychology* 19.1 (2000): 56-69.

Emmons, Robert A., & Teresa T. Kneezel. "Giving Gratitude: Spiritual and Religious Correlates of Gratitude."*Journal of Psychology and Christianity* 24.2 (2005):140- 48.

Finn, J.D. "School Engagement and Students at Risk." *National Center for Education Statistics* Washington, D.C., 1993.

Franklin, John H. *From Slavery to Freedom: A History of African American*. New York: Alfred A. Knop, 1947.

Gilder, George. "The Root of Black Poverty," *The Wall Street Journal*, October 30, 1995.

Gilder, George. "Hope, for the Crisis in Black America," *With Christ.Org*, 2009.

Gorenstein, Peter and Farnoosh Torabi. "Top 5 Tips to Build Wealth and Success", *Saving Smart & Living Well Financially Fit*, October 5, 2010.

Hacker, Andrew. *Two Nations: Black and White, Separate, Hostile, Unequal*. New York: Simon & Schuster, 2003.

Hale, Janice E. *Learning While Black: Creating Educational Excellence in African American Children*. Baltimore: Johns Hopkins University Press, 2001.

Herrnstein, Richard & Charles Murray. *The Bell Curve: Intelligence and Class Structure in American Life*. New York: Free Press, 1996.

Henderson, A. T. and N. Berla. "A New Generation of Evidence: The Family is Critical to Student Achievement." *National Committee for Citizens in Education* Washington, D.C. 1994.

Jacoby, Jeff. "Destruction in Black America is Self-inflicted" *Boston Globe*, September 5, 2007.

James, King. *The Holy Bible*. Nashville: Thomas Nelson Publishers, 1990.

Jones, Shanique. "The Mis-Education of the Negro by Carter G. Woodson" *Associated Content*, June 1, 2007.

Jehrid Mosley. "The Importance of Education in the African American Community." *Blackvoice.com*, 2009.

Judd, Kate. "Gratitude is an Open Door: Three Stories About Wealth and Poverty." *Planet Vermont Quarterly*, Vol. 8 No 3, 2000.

Kashdan, T.B., G. Uswatte, & T. Julian. "Gratitude and Hedonic and Eudaimonic Well-being in Vietnam War Veterans." *Behaviour Research and Therapy*, 44, (2006):*177-199.*

Kurtz, Mary Jo. "Daily thanksgiving: Your Recipe for a Happy Family," *Omaha Family Magazine*, 23, 2009.

Ludwige, Arnold M. *How Do We Know Who We Are?* New York: Oxford University Press,1997.

Massey, Douglas S. and Nancy Denton. *American Apartheid: Segregation and the Making of the Underclass.* Cambridge: Harvard University Press, 1993.

Mathis, Deborah. "The Problem Isn't Credentials; It's Color," *BlackAmericaWeb.Com*, November 29, 2010.

McCullough, M. E., Emmons, R.A & Tsang, J. "The Grateful Disposition: A Conceptual and Empirical Topography." *Journal of Personality and Social Psychology,* 82, (2002). 112- 127.

McCullough, M. E., J. Tsang, & R.A.Emmons. "Gratitude in Intermediate Affective Terrain: Links of Grateful Moods with Individual Differences and Daily Emotional Experience". *Journal of Personality and Social Psychology*, 86, (2004): 295-309.

Miller, Larry. "Changing Our Life Can Be Uncomfortable" *Ground Report*, March, 2009.

Monroe, Irene. "Can Blacks Rid Themselves of the Use of the N-Word?" *The Huffington Post,* August 19, 2010.

Morgan, Lucy. "Gadsden County Government Embroiled in Race Plot Scandal," *St. Petersburg Times*, February 25, 2011.

Murdock, Mike. *The Assignment: Powerful Secrets for Discovering Your Destiny*. Tulsa: Albury Publishing, 1997.

O'Connor, Anahad, "Surgeon General Calls for Health Over Hair" *The New York Times*, Tuesday, August 30, 2011.

Okafor, Victor, "A Reevaluation of African Education: Woodson Revisited." *Journal of Black Studies 22, no. 4, 1992.*

Porter, Judith R. & Robert E. Washington. "Black Identity and Self-esteem: A Review of Studies of Black Self-Concept, 1968-1978." *Annual Review of Sociology*, 1979.

Porteou, Mark. "Crabs-in-a-bucket Theory" *The Human Experience*, March 16, 2010.

Shakur, Assata. "The Destruction of the Black Family" *Freedom Journals*, April, 2007.

Scruggs, Darrick H. & Lisa Bartley Lacey. "Being Black in America," *Ezine Articles*, Dec. 8, 2007.

Small Business Administration. "Minorities in Business", 2001.

Smiley, Tavis. *How to Make Black America Better: Leading African American Speaks Out.* New York: Anchor Books 2001.

Smith, Todd A. "Crabs in a Bucket" *Regal Magazine*, 2010.

Bibliography

Stonequist, Everett V. *The Marginal Man: A Study in Personality and Culture Conflict.* New York: Russell & Russell, 1937

Tsoi-A-Fatt, Rhonda. "African Americans hit hard by poverty spike" *The Grio .Com,* September, 2010.

Unknown Author. "Showing Off", *Progressdaily.Com,* June 13, 2008.

Unknown Author. "Gratitude and Law of Attraction", *Law of Attraction Insight, weekly Newsletter,* June 15, 2011.

Unknown. "Whose Planet Is It Anyway?" *Academic Autistic Spectrum Partnership in Research and Education (AASPIRE) blogspot.com Publication,* February 11, 2008.

Unknown Author. "Addressing Over-representation of African Americans in Special Education." (2002): *National Alliance of Black School Educators,* (Feb. 17, 2007).

Unknown Author. "National Council for Educational Statistics." *NSES 2005 Programs and Plans: Chapter 5 Educational assessment,* 2005.

Wes, Fessler. "Being Thankful in Good and Bad Times," *Family Fun Shop,* November 10, 2010.

Williams, Troy. "Williams: Black Voter Pawns in Political Game" *Fayobserver.com,* August 9. 2010.

Williams, Heather Andrea. *Self-Taught: African American Education in Slavery and Freedom.* Chapel Hill: University of North Carolina Press, 2005.

Wood, A.M., S. Joseph, & P.A. Linley. "Coping Styles as a Psycholigical Resource of Grateful People." *Journal of Social and Clinical Psychology,* vol.*26,* 2007.

Wood, A. M., S. Joseph & J. Maltby. "Gratitude Uniquely Predicts Satisfaction with Life: Incremental Validity above the Domains and Facets of the Five Factor Model." *Personality and Individual Differences, 45,* (2008): 49-54.

Wood, A. M., S. Joseph, & J. Maltby. "Gratitude Predicts Psychological Well- being Above the Big Five facets." *Personality and Individual Differences,* 45, (2009): 655-660.

Woodson, Carter G. *The Mis-Education of the Negro.* Washington D.C.: Associated Publishers, 1933.

Wright, Harold D. "There Are Ways to Help Black Students Succeed in Our Schools." *Tallahassee Democrat,* June 26, 2010.

Yablonsky, L. *The violent gang.* New York, NY: The Macmillan Co, 1962.

About the Author

Dr. Anthony O. Viegbesie is a first-generation American who arrived in the United States of America on September 16, 1978 with practically nothing. Being the first in his family to emigrate from Nigeria to the United States, he started his life as a migrant farm worker harvesting cucumbers, tomatoes, and watermelons along Highway 319 in southern Georgia.

He obtained an Associate of Science in Agriculture from Abraham Baldwin Agricultural College in Tifton, Georgia; a Bachelor of Science in Agricultural Business from Northwestern Oklahoma State University in Alva, Oklahoma; a Master of Science in Agricultural Economics from the University of Kentucky in Lexington, Kentucky; and a Doctor of Philosophy in Public Administration from The Florida State University in Tallahassee, Florida.

He has been a Professor of Economics and Public Administration at Tallahassee Community College,

Tallahassee, Florida and an Adjunct Professor of Economics, Agribusiness, and Public Administration at Florida Agricultural & Mechanical University, Tallahassee, Florida since 1984.

Dr. Viegbesie has also received several special trainings in leadership. He is a graduate of the Florida Educational Leadership Career Advancement Scholars Program, the Leadership Tallahassee Program (Class XIV); and the Citizen Leadership Institute's Citizen Leadership Training Program.

His awards and recognitions include:

- The Florida State Conference of the NAACP's 2000 "Gwendolyn Cherry-Sawyer Award".
- 2000 United States Census "Leadership in Partnership Award" Award"
- The Florida Justice Association's "2003 Consumers' Rights Advocate
- Outstanding Young Men of America, 1985
- Who's Who among Young American Professionals, 1992–1993
- Who's Who in America, 1992
- Who's Who of Emerging Leaders in America, 1993
- Who's Who among American Teachers, 1994

His community and civic involvements include:

- Councilman, Public Safety Coordinating Council, Leon County, Florida, 1998–2009

- Vice-Chair, Tallahassee, Florida, Enterprise Zone Development Agency, 2003–2008
- 1St Vice-President, Florida State Conference of NAACP Branches, 2000 –2008.
- President, Tallahassee Branch, NAACP, 1999 & 2000
- Life Member, Kappa Alpha Psi Fraternity, Inc.
- Golden Heritage Life Member, NAACP

Dr. Viegbesie sees himself as one driven by the need for justice and equality of opportunity for all. His duty is to accentuate the positive and eliminate the negative in the lives and minds of all people of the world. He always invokes the Grace of the Almighty God to guide and protect him as he seeks to complete his assignment here on earth. He dedicates himself to the service of mankind and the improvement of the quality of life for all.

To Contact the Author:
Anthony O. Viegbesie, Ph.D.
P.O. Box 607
Havana, FL 32333
aov@att.net

www.ingramcontent.com/pod-product-compliance
Lightning Source LLC
Chambersburg PA
CBHW062201280526
45788CB00001B/387

*9 7 8 1 4 5 6 4 6 1 8 9 8 *